ALL IS LEAF

A BUR OAK BOOK
Holly Carver, series editor

ALL IS LEAF

Essays and Transformations

JOHN T. PRICE

University of Iowa Press   Iowa City

University of Iowa Press, Iowa City 52242
Copyright © 2022 by John T. Price
uipress.uiowa.edu
Printed in the United States of America

Design and typesetting by Nola Burger

Printed on acid-free paper

Library of Congress Cataloging-in-Publication Data
Names: Price, John, 1966– author.
Title: All is Leaf: Essays and Transformations / John T. Price.
Description: Iowa City, Iowa: University of Iowa Press, [2022]
Identifiers: LCCN 2021045262 (print) | LCCN 2021045263 (ebook) | ISBN
    9781609388355 (paperback) | ISBN 9781609388362 (ebook)
Subjects: LCSH: Price, John, 1966– | Price, John, 1966—Travel. | Price,
    John, 1966—Childhood and youth. | College teachers—United
    States—Biography. | College teaching—United States. | Authorship. |
    Iowa—Biography.
Classification: LCC CT275.P84267 A3 2022 (print) | LCC CT275.P84267
    (ebook) | DDC 378.1/2092 [B] —dc23/eng/20211108
LC record available at https://lccn.loc.gov/2021045262
LC ebook record available at https://lccn.loc.gov/2021045263

For Alden James Gale Price

And my students

Who are we really? What is this life about? I had to learn to become a fool, a barbarian, the moon, a lamppost, a fallen leaf—any angle necessary to answer the question....

—Natalie Goldberg, "Meeting the Chinese in St. Paul"

CONTENTS

My Grant Application Letter (and Introduction):
Concerning This Exceptional Research Project
    1

My Childhood Ghost Story: *The Burnt Plane*
    15

My Rock 'n' Roll Road Song: *Confessions of a*
Prairie Lounge Singer
    18

My Wild Animal Attack Story: *Peacock, Beware!*
    26

My Essay on the Essay: *On Hoagland, Turtles,*
and the Courage of Simile
    32

My Guide to Watching Rankin/Bass Christmas Specials:
Holidays on Green
    40

My Science Fiction Horror Story: *Secret of the*
Ninth Planet (A Weird Tale)
    51

My Graphic Memoir: *The Author with Pipe, in Startlement (By His Four-Year-Old Son, Alden James Gale Price)*
82

My Courtroom Drama: *The Last Case*
85

My Archaeological Dig Site: *Among the Ruins of Bethsaida (On Thirty Years of Teaching Creative Nonfiction)*
108

My Near-Death Experience/Elvis Tribute: *Appendicized*
124

My Break-up Letter: *Dear America*
149

My Arctic Erotica: *Fifty Shades of Grímsey*
154

My Pregame Pep Talks: *The Impossible Season*
176

My Workout Testimonial in the Time of COVID (and Conclusion): *Pizza Night on Planet Fitness*
207

Acknowledgments
223

ALL IS LEAF

MY GRANT APPLICATION LETTER
(AND INTRODUCTION)

Concerning This Exceptional Research Project

Dear Selection Committee Members,

I am writing to formally apply for the Exceptional Research Grant sponsored by your esteemed organization. I'd like to begin by expressing my sincere gratitude for your offer of such generous support for "writers and scholars completing exceptional research projects in the Humanities," and I can confirm that, if my project is selected, the $500 will most certainly assist me in achieving my "professional goals."

Thank you, as well, for participating in the recent online Humanities Research Fair, during which your representative was both friendly and helpful in answering our questions. I admit to some lingering hesitation, however, related to a question someone asked about what sorts of research projects your organization has funded in the past. Your representative explained (again, in a friendly manner) that although the range has been quite large, a distinction should be made in our applications between "serious, scholarly research that can take years to complete" and the "amateurish" kind that involves "simply stepping into your backyard." There were a lot of digital thumbs-up in response to this by attendees, to which I was about to add my own digital thumb, until I recalled that in 2001 *Orion* magazine published an essay of mine titled "Backyard."

It has since occurred to me that a large chunk of my published nonfiction has, in fact, been set in my yard: front, side, and back. I certainly appreciate the need in this political climate, when public funding for the humanities is under such intense scrutiny, to prioritize only the most exceptional and professional research projects. Nonetheless, as I consider how to articulate why you should consider my current research project to be both professional and exceptional, and thus worthy of funding, I feel some trepidation over the recent realization that, despite the best intentions, my project has become, in part, yet another piece *about my yard.*

Still, I will do my best to provide you with the requested "detailed and thorough account of the research process" associated with the project for which I am seeking your support.

The project, titled "All Is Leaf," began several years ago as a serious environmental essay about a centuries-old burr oak tree in our front yard in Iowa, endangered oak savanna ecosystems, and midwestern bioregional ecocide. This tree and our yard, though officially in Council Bluffs, Iowa (pop. 62,000), a town bordering Omaha, Nebraska (pop. 500,000), are part of the Loess Hills in western Iowa—a region of the state where my family has resided for seven generations. This includes my wife, Stephanie, and me and our three sons, in order, Benjamin, Spencer, and Alden. The Loess Hills are, as you might guess, a bunch of hills, which doesn't sound very exceptional. But even a little research reveals that they are unique drifts of loess (German for "loose") soil that piled up here following the final retreat of the glaciers. They run from the north end of the state all the way to the south, into Missouri, and are, in fact, among the last of their kind in the world. They provide refuge for a lot of threatened creatures and ecosystems, like oak savannas, of which this tree in our yard would have once been part.

As I said, this was supposed to be the subject of my research project. Things took an unexpected detour, however, when a good friend from graduate school invited me to attend his fiftieth birthday party in his hometown of Hamburg, Germany, birthplace of the word *loess.* As I considered the possibility of attending, I suddenly became nostalgic for my graduate student days in Iowa City, and, going to the section of my bookshelf dedicated to that nostalgia, picked up *The Sorrows of Young Werther* by Johann Wolfgang von Goethe, which my German friend had given me for my twenty-fourth birthday. As some of you undoubtedly know, it is about a young man who falls in love with an unattainable woman, and as a result becomes depressed and eventually kills himself; but I'd never finished it. This made me feel as if I had somehow failed my friend, whom I'd never once visited in Germany, but should have.

So I decide right there that I am going to Germany, and will finish *Werther*, but I start it all off by visiting Goethe's Wikipedia profile, which for the purposes of this application I do not claim as exceptional research. Nevertheless, it leads me to the discovery that Goethe, who was born in 1749 and died in 1832, was not only the most popular novelist and poet of his time, especially among teenagers, but also a nature writer (like me) and an amateur scientist who made some important contributions to the study of optics, geology, evolutionary science, and botany.

Given the oak savanna essay I am working on, this information intrigues me, and I'm wondering why I haven't heard Goethe mentioned more often among my fellow environmental writers. This leads me to think that a portraiture essay might be both interesting and timely, but to be honest, what I'm actually thinking is that this Germany trip is going to be incredibly expensive—and, since we are basically a one-income family of five, inexcusably selfish—but that I might justify it by publishing said portraiture essay and writing the whole trip off as a tax deduction.

I'll spare you the rest of the practical and emotional details of preparing to leave your spouse and kids for three weeks at the end of a school year and skip ahead to Germany.

After a week spent with my friend and his kids in Hamburg, during which I attend his fiftieth birthday party and share many laughs and memories, I set off alone for a few days of what I intend to be serious, professional research in Goethe's hometown of Weimar. I should confess that until this trip to Germany, I had never been to Europe or anywhere else abroad. The extent of my foreign travels was a tequila run to Nogales, Mexico, with my grandmother when I was fourteen. So when I boarded the plane in Omaha bound for Hamburg, I was full of anticipation, and also a lot of petty and immature fears that I probably should have gotten out of the way by studying abroad in college (as I'm sure several on your committee did). But I was holding down a job during most of my college years and couldn't afford it and still can't afford it when, at age forty-eight, I step off the train in Weimar and am reunited with a more pleasant immaturity that I think is, or should be, a prerequisite of all exceptional research projects: the sense of being a student again.

This may also include, as it does for me, the student's panicked sense of being underprepared. Prior to visiting Weimar I have, in fact, read only the *Werther* book and a couple of articles about Goethe. The rest of my prep time was spent researching decent walking shoes because my middle-aged arches have gone to shit. So although I enter Goethe's hometown with comfortable shoes, I have no true appreciation for the significance of the place—home also to Schiller and Bach and the Bauhaus art movement and the Weimar Republic, Germany's first democratically elected government—and that lack of appreciation at first manifests itself (as it does sometimes for students) in mockery.

For instance, I soon discover that Weimar is home to a bizarre local obsession with gingko trees. While meandering the narrow cobblestone streets, it seems that in every other shop window there are gingko-related items for sale: gingko paintings and sculptures, gingko moisturizing cream, gingko leaf–print jewelry, gingko jam, and so on. We have a big gingko in our front yard, right next to the oak, and for me that tree has always been an interesting, sometimes annoying, botanical sideshow, with its scalloped shell-like leaves, lepidopteron branches, phallic-shaped buds (my boys call it "the penis tree"), and stinking jellied seedpods. More a creature of prehistoric seas than of the native prairies and oak savannas I love.

In Weimar, though, it is clearly something else. Seeking illumination, I enter a little store called Gingko Land and peruse a tiny book (the only one translated into English) entitled *The Gingko Myth*. The author, Heinrich Georg Becker, explains that the gingko had been elevated into German national consciousness by none other than Goethe, who had a scientific interest in the tree and helped introduce the Chinese native to the gardens and parks of Weimar along the willowed banks of the Ilm River. Goethe also wrote a poem, "Gingko biloba," in 1815, which is translated this way in the book:

This tree's leaf which here the East
In my garden propagates,
On its secret sense we feast,
Such as sages elevates.

Is it one but being single
Which as same itself divides?
Are there two which choose to mingle,
So that one each other hides?

As the answer to such question
I have found a sense that's true:
Is it not my song's suggestion
That I am one and also two?

Goethe was sixty-six when he wrote this celebrated but (in my opinion) unexceptional poem, which he dedicated to Marian von Willemer, a thirty-one-year-old banker's wife with whom he shared, in Becker's words, a "secret mutual fondness, never to be fulfilled."

At this point in my research process, however, I am less interested in contemplating Goethe's May–December romantic fantasies than I am in mocking the hyperbolic English translations of Becker's prose about Gingko trees, which I silently read in the voice of Arnold

Schwarzenegger. Lines such as: "endowed with perfect genetical strategies for survival and imbued with archetypal power of great sensitivity" and "it's here too that Gingko's triumphant advance is progressing irresistibly" and "for centuries Ginkgo has been regarded as a source of comfort, spark of hope, power of healing and as a legend having come alive" and "to women visitors they symbolize love and fertility since they remind of reproduction through their naturally-developed individually shaped so-called Chi-Chi-proliferations (Chi-Chi = tit)."

But as I said earlier, this condescension is only a petty and temporary distraction from the humbling realization of how little I know about Weimar and about Goethe, including his apparently famous gingko poem and the immense scope of his mind and influence. That scope becomes pretty clear the next morning, however, when I tour Goethe's residency, the exterior of which is painted a bright yellow, which I notice only because Heinrich Georg Becker suggested it might have been intended to mimic "the shining autumn colors of the Gingko foliage." The house is now a sprawling national museum and the place where I assume I will collect much of the necessary information to complete the portraiture essay for my fellow nature writers and the IRS.

While there, I discover that among Goethe's many and diverse scientific obsessions, plant morphology was near the top. I don't know much about this field but learn from one of the displays that it is the comparative study of physical plant structures and growth, with an emphasis on shared characteristics. There are quotes from Goethe's 1790 book on the subject, *The Metamorphosis of Plants*, in which he expresses a desire to discover "the truth about the *how* of the organism" or, as one scholar puts it, "a unity of form in diverse structures." For Goethe, this underlying unity among plants—the *Urphenomen*—could be found in the leaf. "It came to me in a flash," Goethe wrote, "that in the organ of the plant which we are accustomed to call the *leaf* lies the true Proteus who can hide or reveal himself in all vegetal forms. From first to last, the plant is nothing but *leaf*, which is so inseparable from the future germ that one cannot think of one without the other."

Initially, I'm not entirely sure what this means, only that the idea was immensely influential on other scientists and philosophers, including American transcendentalists Ralph Waldo Emerson and Henry David Thoreau. Thoreau's philosophical take on *The Metamorphosis of Plants*, for instance, might be discerned in this quote from *Walden*:

> You find thus in the very sands an anticipation of the vegetable leaf. No wonder that the earth expresses itself outwardly in leaves, it so labors with the idea inwardly. The atoms have already learned this law, and are pregnant by it. The overhanging leaf sees here its prototype.... The feather and wings of birds are still drier and thinner leaves.... Even ice begins with delicate crystal leaves ... [and] the whole tree itself is but one leaf.... Thus it seemed that this one hill-side illustrated the principle of all the operations of Nature. The Maker of this earth but patented a leaf. What Champollion will decipher this hieroglyphic for us, that we may turn over a new leaf at last?

As I write this quote in my research notebook, it strikes me that the link between Goethe and the god of American nature writing might increase the interest of some environmental magazine editors in publishing my portraiture essay. Their interest might be further piqued by the fact that Charles Darwin was a Goethe fan, long aware of the German's earlier discovery that both humans and monkeys share an intermaxillary bone in the skull, suggesting a biological link many scientists and theologians denied. A reproduction of the skull Goethe used in his research is on display in the museum, as well as the actual instruments (some of them handmade) and detailed drawings used in his other scientific studies, all of them underscoring Goethe's belief that research, in his time, should be verifiable by applying the unaided senses, wedded to personal experience and imagination, and by drawing from materials near at hand.

This included, for Goethe, *the backyard*, where, in his gardens—which are to this day blooming with irises, peonies, and daylilies—he conducted many of his experiments in plant morphology. According to Goethe, all amateurs, if they are careful and disciplined observers as well as creative thinkers, can make original contributions to knowledge. It occurs to me now that this is the way of many essayists, who model a research process that can be replicated not only by those within privileged academic and economic classes, with their access to research libraries and travel funds and relative wealth of time, but by anyone who has the power to bring new attentiveness to what may have previously seemed unexceptional.

Anyone, in short, who is curious.

I'm tempted to say "curious like a child," but that doesn't really capture it, at least not while touring Goethe's home where I encounter instead a surprising adolescent energy that is all too familiar to me, a father of three boys, the two eldest being teenagers. The place is full of rock and fossil collections and reproductions of classical art and shelves of touristy knick-knacks he picked up during his travels. In a couple of upstairs rooms he hosted all-night parties with the rock stars of his time, including Felix Mendelssohn, and a variety of royals. He enjoyed drawing mythological superheroes and hiking outdoors. He loved flirting and hated math. He even had a porn stash, now displayed in a dimly lit side room. This includes a collection of interchangeable coins engraved with erotic images, a vibrantly colored majolica plate portraying Io riding Jupiter, titled *Deep Dish*, and a sketch of a naked foursome going at it inside the petals of an iris—a seemingly ordinary flower found in backyards all over the world.

This is all beside the point of my serious research, I think, so I move on to an area dedicated to "Memories," where an informational sign tells me that Goethe "aims to stage [Weimar] as a center of literature and establishes a culture of remembrance that takes shape in monuments and museums. Up until today, the various institutions such as the library or Goethe's home provide a public forum for commemoration."

This talk of memory, monuments, and museums makes me remember my visit the previous week to the ruins of St. Nicholas Church in Hamburg, destroyed by Allied firebombings in 1943, and the small porcelain portrait there of Goethe, among a glassed-in display of scorched rubble in the museum basement; and then, also, the far back corner of the Weimar Visitor Center where, the day before, I noticed a display of photographs of the Buchenwald concentration camp as I waited in line to purchase a Goethe "Gartenhaus" coffee cup.

To be honest, I hadn't planned to visit Buchenwald because, though Holocaust memoirs had been a major focus of my undergraduate studies in religion, I hadn't realized how close the camp was to Weimar until my Hamburg friend told me so—yet more evidence of my ignorance and lack of preparation. Even then I felt that any visit to a concentration camp should be approached with respectful intention and careful research, so that you don't enter such a place carrying an emptiness that might be too easily filled with nerve-inspired atrocities such as snapping selfies in front of the ovens. Such a visit had to be earned, I thought, and I had not earned it.

Plus, it seemed way off topic. But then, inside Goethe's home, I recall Primo Levi, also a poet and scientist, and his memoir, *Survival in Auschwitz*, which is probably the book most responsible for metamorphosing me into a nonfiction writer and that I first read as a freshman in one of those required humanities courses that are, as mentioned, under such intense scrutiny nowadays. What I think that book taught me, without knowing it, was that witness can be born out of the meeting place between the imperfect, unexceptional individual and the universal, and that it can be inspired and researched and organized, as Levi claimed, out of a personal sense of urgency alone.

So this is how, dear committee members, based on the memory of a book and a vague sense of personal urgency experienced in an eighteenth-century German poet's home, you might find yourself arriving the next day, the same day you had intended to conduct exceptional research at the Goethe and Schiller Archive, at the grounds of Buchenwald concentration camp, having done virtually no preparatory research, intellectually naked, except for whatever information you can accumulate at the information center, which in your case is a map and an audio tour device you are still fumbling with as you approach the iron front gate and the German words that translate into "To Each His Own."

You stop first at the ruins of the zoo, just on the other side of the fence from the crematorium, created (according to the audio tour) by the camp commander for the entertainment of his children and the children of the SS officers who lived there and for the Weimar families, dwelling in the city of music, literature, and commemoration, who regularly visited there, as well, because Buchenwald was promoted as a "family camp." You have a family of your own, of course, and in your community there is also a zoo, with brown bears like the ones cared for here by a young Roma prisoner who likely did not survive, but who left his initials in the concrete of the cave, which you must find, because your children love bears and have left their own initials in concrete elsewhere in the world.

They are now, against your will, there with you, your children, the ones you thought you left behind in Iowa, and for the rest of the day you cannot chase them away. They are there when you enter the Inmates Canteen with the photograph of another young Roma man holding up his sick friend during inspection, because your kids are all about their friends right now. They are there when you see the photo of thin boys behind wire in the Little Camp and the photos of SS officers, also boys, in a camp full of boys who torture and are tortured. They are there when you read the forms ordering these teenage SS boys to submit a racial and religious profile of their fiancées for party approval, and also when you visit the memorial to "homosexual" victims, because you don't know who your boys will love in their time and what commandants they will face.

They are there with you an hour later when you come upon a massive tree stump with a bunch of rocks set on top of it, like the other memorials. When you learn that the prisoners called it Goethe's Oak, you experience a moment of reorientation—*ah, Goethe, trees, research!*—and you think you have finally convinced them to leave, your children, because you do not hear their voices reading the story of how this preserved stump is all that remains of a legendary oak tree, spared by the Nazis because of its superior size when they clear-cut this section of the ancient Ettersberg Forest to build the camp. It was one of the few trees on the grounds, and certainly the most prominent, and though it too was a site of torture, the prisoners called it Goethe's Oak because they believed the great writer himself sat beneath it to compose this poem, bearing the inscription "At the slope of Ettersberg, on 12 Feb '76," which was dedicated to yet another woman Goethe loved but who, as in *The Sorrows of Young Werther*, as in the gingko poem, did not love him back:

> Thou that from the heavens art,
> Every pain and sorrow stillest,
> And the doubly wretched heart
> Doubly with refreshment fillest,
> I am weary with contending!
> Why this pain and desire?
> Peace descending
> Come ah, come into my breast!

You find out that the tree itself was among the final victims of the camp, having been struck by an errant bomb only months before liberation, after which it burned through the night.

You think that is the end of the tree thing in Buchenwald until you visit the art exhibit adjacent to the disinfection chamber and see all the sketches of that same tree by those imprisoned in the camp, so prominent you think you see its twisted limbs, distinctive to oaks, reflected in their sketches of the emaciated limbs of young men, some teenagers, alive and dead—a unity of form in diverse structures. And that's when they return, your own sons, as you consider how much this oak tree, whose ancient cousin grows in your front yard, inhabited the minds and memories of these prisoners, and how it was given that power by a love poem that many of them knew by heart, but that you had until then never read, one that expressed sentiments that, in any other context, such as the willowed banks of the Ilm River or a text message from your teenage son to his almost-girlfriend, you would find unexceptional.

That's when you understand that, whatever it is you intended to research and write, it will no longer be about Goethe, or even the Holocaust, but about how, when everything else is taken or burned away, it is this unexceptional, amateurish, immature love—the *how* of the organism—that keeps your humanity alive.

A week later, you leave Germany, bringing these thoughts, this research, back home to Iowa, to your spouse and your sons, including your teenagers for whom the hope of romantic love is the air they and their friends breathe. You bring them back to the oak tree in your yard, where this all began. Back to the very spot where, on a bright September day—around the same time *Orion* published your "Backyard" essay—you held your firstborn son, Benjamin, barely a year old then, and watched Air Force One fly over those branches on its way to a nearby military bunker in Omaha. In that moment, you understood, for the first time, really, as perhaps they did beneath that other oak tree, that for some powerful people in this world there will always be a safe place to hide when things really go bad, and that those people will likely not include you or the people you love, including the child you are holding.

The oak tree seemed very alone back then, because you felt alone, but now you can't look at it without also seeing its much younger May companion, the gingko. It occurs to you then that such a juxtaposition—gingko and oak, their branches intertwined, leaf touching leaf—is unusual and not something you have truly appreciated before, though you and your family pass by them every day. Including your three boys, who might consider those trees and the yard that contains them to be ordinary, because someone may have told them they are ordinary, that their midwestern place, the Loess Hills, and everything wild that survives here, including themselves, including what they think and feel, in love or in pain—*I am weary with contending!*—is ordinary.

■

With all of this roiling around in the air between us, you can now perhaps appreciate, dear committee members, why I am struggling with how best to conclude this application for your Exceptional Research Grant. How do I summarize what it is I need to explain after all that time spent traveling and reading and writing and thinking and feeling and living and wishing, all of it research, while also acknowledging that I have come to a point in my career, in my life, when I am less concerned with being exceptional than I am with being helpful?

For the record, since returning from Germany five years ago—I know, time flies—my research process has generated more than thirty handwritten notebooks, countless photographs, and well over a thousand typed pages. Some of that research has metamorphosed into writing not directly related to that trip, but still about the same questions. These include drafts and transformations of essays and epistles and satires and memories—stories and forms I've always wanted to write, opinions I've always wanted to express, selves I've always wanted to release, and now need to.

It's a lot, maybe too much—maybe enough to fill a book or two—but this is no age for half-measures. Then again, has there ever been an age that hasn't required of its generations more than they thought capable of giving, of being? As T. S. Eliot (no fan of Goethe) implied in a poem that mentions children and trees and stones and rivers and flowers and fire and love, to appreciate life in its most basic, unexceptional "simplicity" is an effort "costing not less than everything." Nor should it.

Even so, as Eliot also said, "We shall not cease from exploration." By which he meant, I think, there is always more work to do, on the page and in the world, even if that effort does only lead us back home to the people and places, the *backyards*, that have created and re-created us, that we might know them again, "as if for the first time." And ourselves. There are days when I think my particular efforts to do so will amount to something, and then there are days when I think I will set it all aside—not just this research project, but my entire writing life— that I may, as Thoreau once admonished, turn over a new leaf at last.

But then there are those other days, dear committee members, and one may be approaching soon, like next week, when the application for this grant comes due, when I think I will finally abandon all efforts to neatly organize or explain or justify, including this letter, and just scoop it all up, dump it into a box, and mail it to the address of your esteemed organization. Upon opening, the contents—my *everything*— will spill across the oak conference table, along with an unexceptional but sincere note, the words of which are, like the leaf, like the unity of the great *Urphenomen* itself, the only words any writer anywhere has ever written or ever shall write:

Affectionately yours,

John Price

MY CHILDHOOD GHOST STORY

The Burnt Plane

As Jason Murphy's mom drove us to the farm in Moorland, I wondered how it would look now that his dad was dead. It had been almost a year. I pictured man-high weeds and rusty tractors, the house empty, the giant barn rotting with its roof caved in and blackbirds flying out the broken windows. But my first step out of the car was onto freshly mown grass. Jason's uncle was waving from the front porch of the house. We ran past him toward the barn, which was still standing, and slid open the huge doors. Inside, the light from the upper windows shot down through the dusty air, burning leopard spots onto the floorboards. It smelled of oil and wood and hay, like always.

Jason called me over to the space behind the creaky loft stairs. The frame of an old yellow bike rested on the floor, its pieces scattered nearby. Jason planned to fix it up, he said, so he could ride it that summer. Today he was putting on the handlebars and asked me to get the toolbox.

The box, dented and gray, had been set on one of the mismatched workbenches still lining the walls. Its metallic luster stood out against the dust-covered machine parts lying around it. Here and there I could make out handprints in the dirty surface, which were probably his uncle's, but they made me think of Mr. Murphy. Big and dark-haired, part-Sioux he claimed, ace pilot, and WWII hero. Mr. Murphy had always been glad to see me, even after my baby brother died last spring and I spent more time at their farm than usual. He'd never been afraid to put me and Jason, just second graders, to work on one of the junk cars he believed was not yet beyond hope. This kind of work is good for boys, he'd say, and then place impossibly gentle hands on our shoulders, hands that otherwise swallowed everything they touched, including this box, the one I was now somehow lifting on my own.

Jason held the handlebars out in front of him, twisting them right then left, steering through invisible curves. He set them by the bike and pulled a wrench from the toolbox. The wrench was large and grimy, and when it slipped off the nut, Jason's wrist bent toward the floor, but he didn't drop it.

"Don't you miss him?" I asked.

He ignored me, just like the last time I'd asked, and the time before that. He put the wrench down and walked outside. I followed him down the long grassy airstrip to the sheet-metal shed with the tattered windsock on top. We walked around the side, stepping through a thicket of tall grass until we reached what looked like a huge shoebox-shaped something made of interconnected, metal rods.

"This is the plane my dad got killed in," he said, stepping inside the charred, rusty frame. He sat down on the bare steel of the pilot's seat.

I crawled into the space behind him, and sat on the wet grass. The last time I'd seen this plane was in a newspaper photo my mom had shown me a summer ago, its black tail smoking and sticking straight up out of the corn field where Mr. Murphy had been crop-dusting. I was now in that same tail, I guessed, but it was hard to imagine that this—no wings, no propeller, no metal skin—had once been his plane. Grasses and vines were growing up through it.

"I like to sit here sometimes," Jason said with his back to me. "I see things."

I didn't understand, but then I leaned back on my elbows and let my gaze move up the slope of my friend's skull and launch itself over the shed, the barn, and into the atmosphere. Up there, the plane's skeleton vanished, along with my own, until there was nothing but sky. I wondered if this was the same sky Mr. Murphy saw all those times, and the last time. A sky big enough to carry him over any place or time that ever meant something to him—an ancient Sioux hunting ground, a battlefield in France, a cornfield in Iowa. Maybe over our own selves right then, sitting on the ground, looking up.

We stayed there a while, long enough for me to know. Then I followed Jason back to the barn. We had work to do.

MY ROCK 'N' ROLL ROAD SONG

Confessions of a Prairie Lounge Singer

—with thanks to Bob Seger

A few years ago, off a long and lonesome highway, east of Omaha, I gave a reading at a prairie science conference. Ticket holders consisted mostly of state- and county-employed scientists in charge of reconstructing, restoring, and managing the narrow strips of prairie habitat along the roads and highways in Iowa and throughout the Midwest. To appreciate the challenges these people face, you need to understand that only a minuscule percentage of native prairie habitat remains in this region, and it ranks among the most endangered ecosystems in the world. These roadside shreds—otherwise known as "ditches"—control harmful invasive species, reducing the need for herbicides, and are vital, ecological lifelines for many wild creatures, including monarch butterflies.

The conference atmosphere did not convey this significance. The presentations were held in a dim, windowless banquet room at a nondescript hotel on the edge of Interstate 35—I could hear the roar of the semis through the walls. The audience for my reading was a scattered, late-morning group of forty or so who had just sat through a seminar on "Stormwater Interception & Infiltration" and who I knew were dreading yet another go-round with the hotel's pasta buffet. I also knew, because my room shared a thin wall with the conference courtesy room, that more than a few in the audience were hung over from late night partying. A man in the front row had his head resting on his arms, apparently asleep.

Here was the latest in a series of invited readings I'd given for prairie scientific groups during the last few years, including a keynote for an international grasslands conference and a number of regional sympo-siums and prairie dedications. I felt honored to participate in every one of them, and because the sponsoring scientists had continued to invite me back, I'd begun flirting with visions of myself as an interdisciplinary ambassador for the arts, a bridge over the troubled waters between the sciences and the humanities.

As I waited to be introduced at the ditch conference, however, I thought I saw the real truth of it: I had become the lounge singer of the prairie scientific community.

This minor epiphany led my thoughts to wanderin', the way they always do, but this time they landed on larger questions about who I was as a nature writer, questions you'd think I'd have had a handle on by then, such as: For whom do I write, and why?

Then again, ignorance and confusion were nothing new in my rela-tionship to the prairies. While growing up in Iowa, in the heart of what used to be tallgrass wilderness, I couldn't have identified a native stalk of bluestem at gunpoint. That didn't change until the Iowa floods of 1993, when I was a newly married, twenty-something grad student living with my wife in a rural town. As the abandoned fields and un-mowed ditches near our house erupted with native wildflowers and grasses, I bought a field guide and searched hungrily for their names. The enthusiasm I felt for this little bit of prairie wildness carried me out across the region where, during the next year, I hiked and camped in the prairies of South Dakota, Nebraska, and Kansas, and talked with people committed to healing them. That pilgrimage became the subject of my first book, *Not Just Any Land*, and it would end with my first participation in prairie reconstruction efforts in my home state.

Presented this way, my inner transformation from indifference to activism seems simple and complete, but that was not the case. While drawing me into a shaky commitment to the prairies, that initial journey also exposed me to the almost unimaginable extent of their destruction. The grasslands wilderness I had naively imagined encountering no longer existed and never would again. Likewise, I confronted the disappointing fact that I would never be one of those writers who enjoyed a full-fledged love affair with the outdoors. I hated, and still hate, camping. I made serious mistakes during that first trip, such as in South Dakota, when I ignited my kerosene stove in the middle of a gazillion acres of dry grass. That act of stupidity could have led to a massive conflagration, consuming miles of protected habitat. I should have been arrested.

I also made serious mistakes on the page. In one of my earliest efforts at nature writing, I'd casually mentioned that birds have no sphincter muscles, which is something I'd actually heard, and that, given my experiences with birds, seemed a reasonable assumption. The piece had been accepted for publication in a national magazine, but on a whim, I sent it to a nature writer friend for a final read-through. He immediately zeroed in on the sphincter claim and took the liberty of running it by an actual ornithologist, something I perhaps should have thought to do myself. Shortly after, I received an email from the ornithologist with the subject line: "Gross Blasphemy!" He wrote: "Anyone who has ever tried to retrieve and tag turkey buzzard chicks from a tree, while fighting off their parents, knows that birds not only have sphincter muscles, but can use them with deadly accuracy!"

I was more careful with my facts after that, but the sense of myself as an environmental amateur, a fool, a screw-up waiting to happen remained unchanged. As such, I often felt outnumbered by "real" environmentalists, not daring—or deserving—to make a stand.

Thus my early evolution as a nature writer was, like the prairies themselves, fragmented, compromised, and constantly threatened with extinction. My moments of blissed-out communion with wildness had been just that—moments—less like the literary nature shamans

I'd worshipped and more like the ignorant and wayward Christians in a Flannery O'Connor story, who find their right orientation only through fear and violence and humiliation and shame. The surprising thing, however, was that this process had worked; I had grown to love the prairies, no matter how diminished, and at some point I stopped resisting that process in my life and in my writing.

In the title chapter of my next book, *Man Killed by Pheasant and Other Kinships*, I recounted how during that same flooded summer of 1993, while I was barreling down an Iowa highway, a pheasant flew out of a ditch and into my open driver-side window, almost causing me to flip the car—a near-death experience that, like the confrontation with the Misfit in "A Good Man Is Hard to Find," forced me to reconsider the seemingly safe, domesticated landscapes of home. As did the experiences of being swarmed by a herd of wild donkeys on a prairie in South Dakota and being savaged by a supposedly domesticated rabbit hiding behind a neighbor's toilet and watching my first son being born and all of the other unexpected moments of "kinship" with the natural world I recounted in that book.

At some point while writing *Man Killed by Pheasant*, I abandoned all pretense to a consistent voice and consistently linear narrative, in favor of a form that came closer to the midwestern landscape as I'd experienced it: segmented, divided into plots, some a little wilder than others, some smaller or larger, each observed from slightly different points of view, but all interconnected. I also stopped repressing the gallows humor I'd actually used to cope with environmental reality. It was a humor that arose out of my own sense of inadequacy and powerlessness and weakling hope, but which had also allowed me, in turn, to get beyond all that and actually apply whatever miniscule talent I had to serving the land I loved.

Even inside this new personal aesthetic, however, the intent was to connect with readers like me: people who are not scientists, not fully inside environmental commitment, but still struggling to find the door. I was pleased whenever midwesterners told me that something in my writing had inspired them to care about the prairies or some other sliver of remaining wildness, and to become involved in recovery or preservation efforts.

That was the primary purpose of my literary work, I thought. My music.

But what did that music have to offer those who weren't in need of any more reasons to care? These scientists and others were already on the frontlines of restoring and reconstructing the prairies, bit by bit: harvesting and planting the seeds, studying and recording the results, writing the grants, and conducting the difficult, often soul-crushing negotiations with private landowners and corporate farmers and government bureaucracies, including those who controlled the paychecks on which they (and perhaps their families) depended. The people who were in fact sitting—or sleeping—before me at the prairie ditch conference in central Iowa.

What did I really know about them? I had talked with some individually at other events, and the stories of their work never ceased to inform and amaze me. I knew they came from both inside and outside the academic community, from the city and from the country, and that many of them had been working for years to heal native prairie ecosystems the majority of us living in this nation had never seen or known. I also knew that they did not enjoy the luxury of thinking merely in terms of those years. Their vision had to carry a place across decades and centuries, well beyond the boundaries of their own lifetimes. That's how long it would take for their efforts to come to fruition, if ever. I considered their efforts to be a kind of faith, as important as any other, and perhaps best described in the Book of Hebrews: "the substance of things hoped for, the evidence of things not seen."

This sent my thoughts wanderin' again, back to the evangelist who used to visit my college campus every spring when I was an undergraduate. At some point during his animated rant, his wife would inevitably step forward to confess that, until she'd found the Lord, and her husband, she'd been a disco queen who enjoyed casual sex. Perhaps that's the role I was meant to play at this conference, and at others, to serve as witness, because in fact it was true, I had once been a disco king. It was also true that I had once cared nothing for the ravaged prairies of my home and that it wasn't a glorious prairie entire that had transformed that indifference, but the ragged threads that these people had, against all reason, charged themselves to restore and protect.

When the conference director first invited me to participate, he requested that I read my pheasant essay, which he and a number of other attendees had heard and enjoyed at previous events. Truth be told, it was my biggest hit. Out there in the spotlight, however, I sized up the situation and decided to begin by telling the audience, somewhat awkwardly, how much I sincerely loved ditches and how often they appeared in my books. There were, for example, the ditches where I first learned to identify native plants after the floods; and the ditches where that doomed pheasant had lurked before flying into my car; and the ditches outside the farmhouse we once rented, a grassy wilderness sheltering bobwhites and snakes and the occasional pack of beer-drinking teenagers, makin' night moves.

I asked them to consider all the people who were, at that very moment, driving by their restored prairie roadsides and pausing for a second, in their minds, to admire the wildflowers and grasses, to feel what we always feel in the presence of natural beauty—wonder, wholeness, joy—before continuing on their way. Like the margins in a photograph, their memories of those prairies would fade, but as most of us know, once a little wildness is allowed into a place, and into the human heart, it cannot be extracted easily. We carry it with us always, and no matter how far we roam, it calls us back to a community we no longer entirely define by the artificial boundaries so often used to divide us from one another and from the earth. When it is possible to return to the ecological community, even briefly, even when barreling down a highway at 70 mph, against the wind, we return, as Wendell Berry puts it, not only "to a renewed and corrected awareness of our partiality and mortality, but also to healing and to joy in a renewed awareness of our love and hope for one another. Without that return we may know innocence and horror and grief, but not tragedy and joy, not consolation or forgiveness or redemption."

"For many of us living here in prairie country," I told them, "you are the founders and stewards of that redemptive community and on behalf of its citizens, I thank you."

The audience stared at me blankly, apparently unmoved, except for the man in the front row who rolled his drowsy head from one arm to the other. It kind of made me feel a million miles away. So I surrendered and began, once again, to read the story of the pheasant that flew into my car, a story that, to tell the truth, had started to bore me, but one that these scientists kept requesting at their gatherings and who laughed at it harder and longer than any other kind of audience. They did so again this time, even the guy in the front row, and afterward the conference director asked if I would consider speaking to them again in the future. The whole thing was beyond me.

Turn the page.

■

Driving home, I didn't pay much attention to the roadside prairies, which were undoubtedly in full summer bloom. I was too busy trying to stay awake. I had, as mentioned, been up late the previous night, listening to the scientists party in the neighboring room and in the hallway. A shared door was located near my head. Through the loud, classic rock track—Joplin, The Stones, Seger—I overheard pieces of increasingly passionate conversations about shrinking budgets and swelling bureaucracies and annoying administrators. About frustrating scientific riddles and debates about the answers and the needs of this or that prairie place versus another. About losses and failures and hard-earned successes and wondering if any of it would make a difference or if they'd ever fall in love with someone who was worth a damn or, at the very least, gave a damn. The evening's festivities were punctuated by someone vomiting just outside my room.

As I'd listened to the retching the night before, I hadn't thought much beyond how gross it was, but now, back on the road again, I saw it as a sign that whatever else these people might be—a people of science or faith—they were also a people in despair. Unlike most of us living here, there were no ecological facts or depressing statistics or cataclysmic predictions or naïve and sentimental hopes these people hadn't already confronted. Like amplifiers, it all echoed in their heads. They weren't in need of that kind of nature writing, from me or anyone else. What they were in need of, finally, was a little laughter. A little song and revelry.

And I think they knew just the fool who could pour it out for them, as natural as sweat. Or the music that he made.

MY WILD ANIMAL ATTACK STORY

Peacock, Beware!

These cats are predators that cause problems for humans.... I have been considering hunting a mountain lion. I am curious what the meat tastes like, and I would love to have one mounted in my living room. There is room for all of God's creatures right next to the mashed potatoes on my plate.
—Letter to the Editor, Omaha World-Herald, January 7, 2014

Guess what we saw on the bus home, Dad? A peacock walking across the road with a bunch of turkeys—we all freaked out!
—Spencer Price, author's son, age nine

COUNCIL BLUFFS, IOWA (AP) — Citizens of this community on the banks of the Missouri River are in an uproar over recent sightings of a free-roaming, feral peacock. The presence of the bird, a large male, has excited local imaginations but also raised concerns about safety and whether this populated area, long empty of most of its native wildlife, is prepared to host such an unpredictable and potentially dangerous animal.

"This is a serious situation," said Dan Chalmers, a conservation officer with the Iowa Department of Natural Resources (DNR). "Sure, peacocks are pretty, and we've all enjoyed seeing them on TV, but does anyone know how they behave in the wild? We have no idea what to expect."

Part of Chalmers's concern arises from a nearly fatal encounter last month with a family of five on their way to the grocery store—the first reported peacock sighting in the area.

"It was my day with the kids, OK, and we were totally out of Mountain Dew," said parent Julie Novotny. "So I throw the boys in the minivan and about half-way along that little stretch of woods across from the high school, this giant blue-green monster explodes out of the trees and shoots across my windshield. Next thing we're screaming our heads off and I'm weaving all over the road—I seriously almost flipped the van! When I finally pulled over, there it was: a huge peacock, not five feet away and all puffed-up like the Fourth of July, glaring at us. That's when I called 911."

By the time police arrived, the bird had fled, but its proximity to the school prompted District Superintendent Carla Montrose to cancel classes for the rest of the week. Council Bluffs mayor Todd Calhoun feels Montrose's actions were justified, and although there have been no reported attacks, he and other city officials continue to urge caution.

"It's all about respecting the wild nature of this animal," Calhoun said. "I've been told peacocks possess very sharp beaks and foot spurs, and aren't afraid to use them. So it's important to keep the kids and pets close to the house, especially at dusk, and to make loud noises when taking out the garbage. If confronted, you should make yourself large by lifting your arms above your head and back away slowly. Don't run, as that may trigger its chase instinct, and whatever you do, don't look into the multitude of eyes on its tail feathers as you could become paralyzed with fear."

Chalmers agreed that citizens should take reasonable precautions and cited recent DNR research into the history and temperament of this species.

"Apparently, the male is officially called a peafowl and is native to India. According to Hindu tradition, the god of war rode a peacock into battle, which should tell you everything you need to know about its disposition," said Chalmers.

While it is unclear how such a large, colorful, and aggressive avian predator could remain undetected for so long in this urban area, Chalmers referenced a recent sighting by a school bus driver of the peacock cavorting with a gang of wild turkeys. He believes the turkeys could be providing the fugitive with food and protection.

"They may consider the peacock one of their own kind," Chalmers said. "Or some version of what they want to be, like a movie celebrity or a god. Personally, I suspect it's nesting somewhere down by the casinos, where it can blend in. That's what I'd do."

The question of why the peacock has chosen the Council Bluffs area as home remains a mystery. Although just across the Missouri River from Omaha, Nebraska, a metropolitan area of nearly half a million, Council Bluffs is located within the Loess Hills of western Iowa, an internationally unique natural area that contains most of what remains of the state's original prairies and savannas. Even so, the hills continue to be excavated for development and used as landfill. Lewis and Clark and other early explorers to the area observed a wilderness replete with large native animals, including bison, bear, elk, and wolves, all of which were exterminated by the end of the nineteenth century. Their return appears unlikely. Iowa currently has less than one-tenth of one percent of its native habitats remaining, the lowest percentage in the US.

Recently, however, mountain lions have been following hunting routes from Wyoming and the Black Hills of South Dakota back to the Missouri River Valley, where the species once resided for centuries. A few have been spotted in eastern Nebraska and western Iowa, prompting front-page articles and warnings in area newspapers and on radio and television, though there have never been any reported mountain lion attacks on humans in the area. Annually, more Americans die from being charged by cattle than nearly the entire number killed by mountain lions in North American during the last one hundred years, which is less than two dozen.

Unlike mountain lions, the peacock is not native to Iowa, but one theory suggests it may be taking advantage of an ecological opportunity created by the near complete elimination of indigenous species and the habitats that once supported them. This poses a unique population control problem, according to Chalmers.

"Peacocks have no known natural predators, not even humans, so right now this bird is perched at the top of the food chain," said Chalmers. "With the mountain lions, we know from experience that most of those in Iowa will be hit by vehicles or shot dead on sight. Across the river, the Nebraska Game and Parks Commission recently opened a hunting season for the twenty or so lions in that state, and we're currently reviewing a public petition asking that we do the same here with peafowl. That decision is pending, but either way, something's going to have to be done for the sake of public safety. And I have a message for Mr. Fancy Feathers: it may not be pretty."

Ty Milner, the author of the DNR petition and resident of nearby Crescent, Iowa, says he and other local hunters are more than ready to collaborate with state officials on establishing a limited hunting season for peacock.

"Hunters are by definition conservationists," said Milner, "and this is clearly a conservation challenge we can assist with. Now, I've never eaten peacock, but I was reading on the internet that Medieval kings used to serve them and swans at royal banquets. I've actually eaten swan and let me tell you, it's good stuff, so I trust those guys. Plus my wife thinks a peacock will make a more stylish wall hanging above the couch than the Arkansas boar's head I've got up there now. It's a win-win for everyone."

Although the fate of this particular bird remains uncertain, some residents are hoping it remains in the area, citing the need for a new injection of wildness into the life of the community and the potential for attracting ecotourist dollars.

"This peacock could be the biggest thing to happen to Council Bluffs since local girl Farrah Abraham appeared on MTV's '16 and Pregnant,'" said chamber of commerce member Bea Dandridge. "Do you know how long it's been since we've had a decent wild animal to put on a t-shirt around here? Deer have been done to death, and we're all getting a little tired of watching them eat our ornamental hostas. So have black squirrels, which are kind of the town mascot, but technically they're a rodent. After that, we're looking at the mosquitoes out on Mosquito Creek and some endangered creature living in the Loess Hills, a toad or skink or something. That's just never going to sell."

Local children also seem excited about the mysterious stranger from the wild, despite the fears and warnings of grown-ups. Noah Tyler, twelve, who claims to have witnessed the peacock strutting across his backyard, hopes it will stick around.

"When I first saw it, I was playing zombie *Black Ops*, but I just dropped the controller and ran to the window," said Tyler. "Dude, that thing was cool with its tail all up and its hundred eyes staring at me like the Wart Boss in *Zelda: Majora's Mask*. And have you, like, seen *Kung Fu Panda 2*? The peacock warrior in that movie kicked some serious butt! I've been looking out the window for it ever since and even went outside a couple times but haven't seen anything."

"I think the peacock may be kind of sad and lonely," said Denisha Crosby, ten, "and I hope no one hurts it. One time I heard it at night, because its voice is really loud and screechy and not like anything else I've heard in my backyard. It sounded like it was crying, 'Help! Help!', but I didn't know if it needed help or if it was saying someone else needed help or what I was supposed to do. And no one around here can really tell me."

Whether help for the peacock is forthcoming, and what form it will take, is yet to be determined. Another petition circulating has called on the DNR and city of Council Bluffs to take measures to sedate and transfer the bird to a safe facility, such as nearby Henry Doorly Zoo in Omaha, which has experience with wildlife rehabilitation. In 2003, zoo staff captured a male mountain lion that had been shot in the leg by a startled police officer in Omaha. After healing from its injuries, the lion—now popularly called "Omaha"—was moved to an enclosure in the zoo's cat complex, where it remains today for visitors to admire.

"That might be a possibility in this case," said Chalmers, "but like I said, public well-being comes first. If the peacock is captured alive, I'm not opposed to locking it behind glass at the zoo, where it would certainly receive the royal treatment it seems to think it deserves. Who knows, maybe they could put him in a cage next to old Omaha, to help educate young people about the natural history of this area. Not enough of them appreciate that nowadays."

MY ESSAY ON THE ESSAY

On Hoagland, Turtles, and the Courage of Simile

—for Ned Stuckey-French

Early in my training as a nature essayist, I was taught to avoid certain kinds of simile like the plague. I was told that to imply, either directly or indirectly, that members of another species are like something or someone else, or that they think or feel as humans do (aka anthropomorphizing), invited a dangerous disrespect for the needs of other species, which can be radically different from our own. That was true, as well, for entire ecosystems such as the prairie wilderness of my home region, which was described by early white explorers as being "like" a desert or "like" an ocean, anything but itself, and thus ultimately transformed to be "like" yet another something—an eastern forest, a beanfield, a suburb, a wind farm, a vein of ethanol. Now most of that prairie wilderness is like, well, nothing at all.

Despite this, I have repeatedly violated the simile rule, especially when it comes to animals. I blame Edward Hoagland's "The Courage of Turtles," which my late friend Ned Stuckey-French introduced to me when we were in graduate school together in the 1990s. I was in my early twenties, and from the moment I first read that essay, it completely disarmed me. It broke down boundaries, decimated the nature writing rulebook, and set me off on wild tangents that at first invited, but ultimately defied, easy understanding—just as, according

32

to Hoagland, good essays should. "Essays don't usually boil down to a summary, as articles do," he wrote in "What I Think, What I Am." They are, instead, "a combination of personality and originality and energetic loose ends that stand up like the nap on a piece of wool and can't be brushed flat."

"The Courage of Turtles" has this kind of nap, and no matter how many times I read it or teach it, which is a lot, I can never quite comb it flat, though I continue to try.

As Ned informed me, the essay was originally published on December 12, 1968, in the *Village Voice*, but that meant nothing to me. What did matter, at least at first, was that it was about turtles. At the time, my future wife, Stephanie, and I shared custody of an eastern box turtle named Methuselah, so I was moved right away by Hoagland's description of how turtles and other wildlife were displaced (or killed) when a pond near his boyhood home was bulldozed to make it flow "like an English brook." I had been feeling a little guilty about purchasing a turtle at a pet store, but felt momentarily vindicated by this sad story and by Hoagland's claim that turtles "manage to contain the rest of the animal world." Saving them, as he suggested, could thus become a major "case of virtue rewarded," and he used a ton of similes to compare turtles to, among other vulnerable creatures, giraffes, warhorses, hippos, penguins, puppies, elephants, turkeys, and cow moose.

I would have added that turtles are also like hermit crabs, full of surprises, such as the day when Methuselah appeared to be excreting all of his internal organs out his backside—a huge, wet tube of purple, pink, and amber. Panicked, I called the vet who, after conducting additional research, informed me that Methuselah was simply experiencing "arousal." Prior to that, I had not considered turtle sexuality as anything more interesting than two rocks knocking together. Now I thought of it as being like the colors of a sunset or a tropical flower or a circus clown hat.

This is the kind of wild tangent I'm talking about when I talk about reading "The Courage of Turtles"—I mean, who needs it? I did, apparently. As a midwestern nature writer, living in a state where so little actual wild nature remains, I was just beginning to understand that I would have to do a lot with a little, and Hoagland's essay was a good model. The list of my own animal obsessions was fairly short at the time, and decidedly non-native, but his piece encouraged me to take stock.

The earliest was tigers—a fascination shared, as it happens, by Hoagland. "We have wiped tigers off the earth," he wrote in "The Problem of the Golden Rule," "and yet our children hear as much about the symbolism of tigers as children did in the old days." I was one of those children. My maternal grandparents called me "Tiger" and gave me all kinds of tiger stuff, such as a tiger sleeping bag and tiger slippers and tiger pajamas and tiger posters with which I papered my bedroom walls in Fort Dodge, Iowa. I was a small, physically awkward kid who mostly hung out alone in his room, so I suppose tigers symbolized everything I wasn't: powerful, confident, beautiful, graceful. During that same period, my grandparents regularly took me to the now defunct restaurant chain Sambo's, where wall murals depicting the Lil' Sambo story taught me that tigers could also be a lot like racism.

I often wonder if that early obsession with tigers led to my more recent obsession with mountain lions, which are returning to their home territory here in the Loess Hills of western Iowa and facing a tough time of it. Hoagland wrote about his own obsession with the species in "Hailing the Elusory Mountain Lion," and why I don't teach that essay more often, I can't say. Perhaps it's because my experiences with animals here in the Midwest have, for most of my life, been less about respecting their wild freedom than the ethical conundrums associated with creatures over whom we have complete control. Cows and pigs, for instance. Also, domestic pets—that kind of power relationship with animals (as Hoagland's essay testifies) offers up its own distinct set of responsibilities, personal associations, and similes.

In kindergarten I owned a couple of painted turtles, Jack and Jill, but was forced to "set them free" in a nearby stream, on the verge of winter, because my mother had heard on the radio that turtles can be like *Salmonella*. Most of the hamsters I owned escaped and ended up dead in the old coal room in our basement, which, I guess, was like some kind of elephant graveyard for hamsters. In first grade, I fell in love with a calico guinea pig named Peppermint Patty, but then my teacher convinced my parents that it would be fun and informative to mate Patty with her own monstrous white guinea pig, Snoopy, which she kept in the classroom. Patty and her pups died during birth not long before my only brother died during birth, which became its own unfortunate simile.

Perhaps because of this, I temporarily moved away from relationships with flesh-and-blood animals and, in the fourth grade, became infatuated with a rubber spider monkey purchased at a dime store. I named him Linus, safety-pinned him to my shoulder, and wore him to school for a couple of days. There I learned that spider monkeys were a lot like public humiliation.

As a grown-up nature writer, I have, like Hoagland, explored obsessive relationships with numerous wild and domestic creatures in my published work. These include bison, mice, pheasants, squirrels, praying mantids, falcons, cannibalistic Triops (misleadingly advertised in the 1970s to be like "sea monkeys"), daddy longlegs, woodchucks, moles, elk, brown recluse spiders, prairie dogs, monarch butterflies, roaches, hummingbirds, robins, frogs, and children.

I am currently obsessed with peacocks. In writing about these creatures, I have rationalized that my anthropomorphizing and liberal use of simile are less about arrogant assumptions and more about trying to create in the reader what Hoagland refers to in "What I Think, What I Am" as "a golden empathy"—though he claims such empathy is primarily the stuff of fiction, not the essay. Or maybe what Buddhists call *pratītyasamutpādu*, the interconnection of all things, which implies not only complete dependence on the well-being of other life-forms but also the necessity of humility, even in the wake of what we think at first is knowledge.

While arguing that "our loneliness" makes us avid essay readers, Hoagland claims that essays themselves "belong to the animal kingdom." As such, they often elude easy capture or containment, which is how it should be when a nature essay—or an ecosystem—is working well. Inside such a place, on the page or on the earth, people think they are chasing down one kind of animal, one kind of knowledge, but then an almost-connection leads them to another and another, until the meaning and responsibility for that meaning lands back in the collective lap of our own species, in our own historical ways with one another.

This is part of the brilliance of "The Courage of Turtles," as I've experienced it, but I didn't fully appreciate that until I was preparing to teach it in one of my writing classes as a graduate teaching assistant. I was once again puzzling over the ending, where Hoagland describes an aquatic terrapin that he rescued but ultimately found "exasperating" because it exhibited "none of the hearty, accepting qualities of wood turtles." In a well-meaning, but botched, "born free" moment, Hoagland tosses the terrapin off a New York pier, only to realize that the water was too deep, the currents too strong, and that the turtle would likely die. The essay concludes: "But since, short of diving in after him, there was nothing I could do, I walked away."

This scene, when I initially read it, seemed a powerful statement about the human relationship to the natural world. Here was an example of the dangerous limits of our knowledge, and the even more dangerous limits of our ability to risk true identification with other living beings, because of what it might require of us. The danger of simile, perhaps.

But then, probably because I was about to teach the piece and felt some additional pressure to be thorough, I reconsidered the publication date, 1968, and an entirely new set of associations presented themselves. I went back through and took note of Hoagland's description of a captive turtle as having a "swollen face like a napalm victim's" and also this description of the turtles fleeing Mud Pond: "Creeping up the brooks to sad, constricted marshes, burdened as they are with that box on their back, they're walking into a setup where all their enemies move thirty times faster than they. It's like the nightmare most of us have whimpered through, where we are weighted down disastrously while trying to flee; fleeing our home ground, we try to run."

Later, when I shared these observations with my students, I had the luxury of watching them conclude on their own and fairly quickly that this essay was not just about turtles but maybe also about the Vietnam War and empathy for its victims, civilian and military. This was the early nineties, and some of their family members were veterans of that war, or, like me, had heard people talk about those they knew, even loved, who'd been emotionally or physically injured, been killed, or suffered mental illness. After further discussion, some of the students concluded that the final scene might also be suggesting that the American government would, in the interests of protecting itself, walk away from Vietnam and those it was supposedly going to "free." Those it had promised, at the very least, to protect. Including our returning soldiers.

In this way, we discovered that an essay could be a lot like prophecy.

But time, like nature, cannot be contained, and my teaching experiences with "The Courage of Turtles" have roamed dramatically in the last twenty-five years. Nowadays, when I mention 1968 and napalm and ask my students for their associations, far fewer of them volunteer anything specific about Vietnam. This inevitably disappoints me; but this disappointment, because I invite and expect it, is likely nothing more than cheap compensation for growing older. The history lesson I now feel compelled to deliver, though important in its own way, too often allows the delusion that the large-scale, murderous forms of hubris I knew in my youth, during that wartime, are in some essential way different from those known by my young students in this wartime.

Setting up such a generational hierarchy risks becoming, for an aging professor, yet another case of virtue rewarded, a chance to "free" students from their own ignorance. This supposedly heroic effort leaves less time to confront the still urgent, uncompromising fact that we remain at our most dangerous when we think we know what's best for another being, making reckless, even fatal assumptions about how they should live or feel or mate or believe or know. Whether that being is another species or another person sitting across a classroom or halfway across the globe.

Still, I can't help myself. Case in point, my current obsession with writing about peacocks. Or rather, a particular male peacock that has been seen running around our wooded neighborhood with a gang of wild turkeys. He was first spotted a few years ago by my then nine-year-old son, Spencer, crossing the road in front of his school bus— a strutting riot of blue and green amid the dull colors of his adopted clan. The peacock and turkeys have been spotted many times together since then, by many people, and on certain spring mornings, his high-pitched screech—*Help! Help!*—has shattered the otherwise trickling, zen-like music of the songbirds leaking in our bedroom windows.

In the stunned silence that usually follows, I can't resist wondering if that peacock feels vulnerable or lonely, or perhaps rebellious or brave. Does it take courage for a peacock to run with a gang of turkeys, to attempt to be *like* a turkey? Is he a living example of the courage of simile, the grammatical expression of the desires and actions of a creature who needs, for whatever reason, to overcome his isolation and connect with another species, another being—to be like another, and therefore, in some way, *become* another? To transform inside, making their needs his own? Or if those needs are beyond understanding, to at least make their fate his own?

To finally, and without hesitation, dive in?

The questions and challenges presented by this kind of "golden empathy" seem as relevant today as they were in 1968 or, say, the day Jesus was born. But will future readers of my peacock story see it that way? I'm a bit worried about that, about future readers, because I'm not sure I'll have any. If I do, I kind of both love and hate to think about somebody teaching my essay and saying something like, "Yes, it may seem to be a vapid piece about a peacock running wild around his neighborhood, but look at the publication date! What does that year in America mean to you, class? It was, of course, the year of the government shut-down, the closing of our national parks, the birth of Obamacare and the death of Andy Griffith—but also the Boston Marathon bombing and the devastating tornadoes in Oklahoma and our endless wars in the Middle East. It's all there in Price's essay if you look closely!"

Will anyone care enough to look that closely and see all of these things? If so, will they also see through the camouflage of historical relevancy to what Hoagland has designated as the true subject of all essays: "The fascination of the mind"? Will they see—do I want them to see—that the real reason the author first became fascinated with that singular peacock is that it seemed funny and out of place and in its pathetic self-deception, almost, but not quite, graceful? And that the year 2013 was, among other things, the year when the author, moving toward fifty, was especially appreciative of all things funny, out of place, pathetic, and almost-but-not-quite graceful.

Sort of like him.

MY GUIDE TO WATCHING RANKIN/BASS CHRISTMAS SPECIALS

Holidays on Green

Peter Roth, Chairman
CEO, Warner Bros. Television
4000 Warner Blvd.
Burbank, CA 91501

December 15, 2012

Dear Mr. Roth,

I am writing as a father and environmentalist to express concerns about your annual Rankin/Bass holiday special lineup. Please accept my apology if I am addressing the wrong corporation—the rights to these shows have been passed around more times than a misfit toy, so it's hard to keep track. What isn't hard to keep track of is the way these shows have spread environmental misinformation among America's children!

Case in point, just last week my three-year-old son, Alden, and I were outside observing some deer in our backyard. We have yet to get any snow or severe cold thanks to climate change, but that didn't delay these white-tailed locusts from making their annual migration onto our property to eat everything they'd forgotten to eat during the preceding months, which wasn't much. While watching them strip the bark off the peach tree, Alden asked, "When will the deers start flying?"

That's a strange question, I said to myself, especially for someone who will supposedly be entering preschool in less than a year. I calmly corrected him that deer (pl.) can't fly.

His response—"Why?"—was expected. It was the same response I'd gotten from his two older brothers when I'd stopped them from jumping off the garage with gliders they'd made out of cardboard boxes. They'd whined and complained, of course, but I feel strongly that one of the core principles of good parenting is introducing otherwise happy children to the laws of physics.

Such was the case here, I thought, so I further explained to him that deer (pl.), unlike birds, possess neither wings nor hollow bones. I thought that would settle the matter, but the look on my son's face revealed disappointment that seemed to border on the quasi-existential —and that was before the tears.

I quickly took him inside where his mother made him a cup of hot chocolate, during which he just kept blubbering, "Rudolph. Rudolph. Rudolph." Stephanie informed me that Alden had recently watched the *Rudolph the Red-Nosed Reindeer* DVD his grandmother had given him as an early Christmas gift, in which reindeer (pl.) do indeed fly. It was the very same program she and my father had introduced to me as a child in the 1960s. Back when it was shown only once a year, limiting the scope of the damage.

You may think this experience with my son is funny, but let me invite you to reflect: Are you and your stockholders ready to assume responsibility for propagating fake science in an era when climate change and environmental ignorance are widely known to be the biggest threats to life on this planet, including the survival of our own species? If our descendants are to have any future at all, we need facts, not fable!

In that spirit, I'd like to offer my assistance.

After rewatching many of these holiday specials—let's call it "field research"—I have drafted an educational guide that I think will be helpful to your viewers, especially those raising impressionable children. It will be fair, as well, reflecting my belief that these programs are not entirely devoid of environmental wisdom and practical advice. Last but not least, the style will be accessible to a general audience, seasonal, and even fun. Who says environmentalists always have to be party-poopers?

For each case study, I have selected a representative scene and organized my analysis into "nice" and "naughty" environmental lessons for parents to discuss with their children, perhaps over cups of hot chocolate. Here are some examples:

1. In *Rudolph the Red-Nosed Reindeer* (first aired December 6, 1962), prospector Yukon Cornelius, while exploiting natural resources for his own financial gain, returns to Christmas Town along with the recently de-fanged Abominable Snow Monster of the North. Both had fallen into a crevasse and were presumed to be dead. "Didn't I tell you?" Yukon exclaims to the surprised elves. "Bumbles bounce!"

LESSONS:

Nice: Yukon rightly scolds the citizens for lacking biological knowledge about a large and, despite its craving for deer-meat (when no pork is available), wrongly vilified, native predator.

Naughty: Taming or removing large predators from their natural habitats will have no long-term negative consequences. In fact, these creatures wish to stop preying on other animals in order to serve a more useful role in the human, Elvish, and/or anthropomorphic communities, such as placing stars on Christmas trees.

2. In *Frosty the Snowman* (first aired December 7, 1969), Frosty and his young friend Karen (who is freezing to death in her skirt) happen upon a poinsettia-filled greenhouse in a remote, possibly subarctic forest. After Karen and Frosty enter, an evil magician locks the door and Frosty melts.

LESSONS:

Nice: Artificial habitats, such as Biosphere II and Walmart Garden Centers should be approached with serious skepticism.

Naughty: In severe wilderness conditions, help will always be available to the reckless and underprepared.

3. In *Santa Claus Is Comin' to Town* (first aired December 14, 1970), a young Kris Kringle befriends Topper the penguin and other animals who teach him important skills and endearing mannerisms (he jumps "as high as a deer" while fleeing the Burgermeister Meisterburger and learns from seals how to laugh "ho-ho-ho!").

LESSONS:

Nice: As scientists have demonstrated, our physical and psychological well-being is dependent on close contact with wildlife.

Naughty: Wildlife is valuable only insofar as it benefits our physical and psychological well-being. Also, that it is possible to encounter penguins and seals in the German Alps.

4. In *The Year Without a Santa Claus* (first aired December 10, 1974), Mrs. Claus seeks to cheer Santa and win a personal bet by causing it to snow in the sunny Zone 9 community of Southtown. Failing to convince Snow Miser and Heat Miser to temporarily exchange territorial dominion, she complains to Mother Nature, who commands her "boys" to honor Mrs. Claus's request.

LESSONS:

Nice: Weather is a complex, often-volatile balance of atmospheric extremes.

Naughty: Those extremes can and should be manipulated to satisfy human desires.

These are just a few examples—I've got a lot more ready to share, not all of them Christmas themed. In fact, I've found the other Rankin/ Bass holiday specials equally complex, if not more so. This would include the feature-length film *Mad Monster Party?* (1967), which portrays android sex slavery and ends with nuclear genocide. The less said about that one, the better.

Then there is *The Leprechauns' Christmas Gold*, first aired on December 23, 1981, but which I assume was intended to cover St. Patrick's Day, as well, perhaps to cut costs. It might also cover Arbor Day, since the story begins with Irish cabin boy, Dinty Doyle, digging up the lone pine tree on an island of native Leprechauns. Like all such ignorant destruction, it unleashes a terrible chain of events, beginning with the release of the screaming banshee, Mag the Hag. Mag is clearly an embodied, inappropriately gendered metaphor for extreme weather, creating hurricane-force storms and catastrophic flooding. To survive, she requires Leprechaun gold, given willingly, or else she turns into tears and vanishes.

Substitute "Leprechaun gold" with "federal subsidies for industrial polluters" and "Banshee tears" with "tears shed by the millions of people poisoned, impoverished, displaced, or outright killed by greed-driven environmental degradation" and you may have yourself an eco-dystopic classic rivaling *The Lorax*, *Avatar*, or even *Soylent Green*.

Unfortunately, *Here Comes Peter Cottontail* (first aired April 4, 1971) spends most of its storyline oversimplifying the physics of time travel, via Seymore S. Sassafras's "Yestermorrowbile," while also stigmatizing a psychologically damaged rabbit amputee named January Q. Irontail and his fruit bat companion, Montresor. The latter may be, in fact, a Greater Mascarene flying fox—a species designated "endangered" by the IUCN.

Perhaps as a corrective, Rankin/Bass released *The Easter Bunny Is Comin' to Town* in 1977. This time, the main villain is a giant grizzly bear named Gadzooks, who attacks orphan children until those same children pacify him with the gift of a snappy Easter suit and hat. From the "naughty" angle, this story is a blatant biophiliac fantasy. From the "nice" angle, it might facilitate a meaningful conversation between religious parents and their children about how God intended us to share the Earth with animals who have every right to maim and/or eat us.

Adult Rankin/Bass viewers might have additional questions unrelated to religious or environmental issues, which have nevertheless haunted them since childhood—I know I do! For instance, the opening credits for many of these shows laud "the talents of Paul Frees." Who is this Mr. Frees and what are these talents? I know he is the voice for many of the Animagic puppets, including Burgermeister Meisterburger, but the plural suggests something more, something multiple, maybe even interdisciplinary. Did he, for instance, run a chemistry lab out of his garage or make Amish-style furniture or publish a collection of nature essays?

Speaking of mysterious, the voice for Gollum in the Rankin/Bass animated production of *The Hobbit* (1977) is credited to "Theodore." As a youngster who loved this movie, but who suffered nightmares narrated by Theodore's voice, I frequently asked myself: Why only the one name? Is he the Devil? Later I found out that he was a comedian named Theodore Isidore Gottlieb, who someone quoted on Wikipedia describes as "Boris Karlov, Surrealist Salvador Dali, Nijinsky, and Red Skelton... simultaneously."

Here, apparently, is also a man of many talents—but are they as numerous as those of Paul Frees? Viewers need to know. Especially those, like me, who are prone to insomnia.

Now, I don't want to leave the impression that I have a personal issue with Rankin/Bass productions. I realize they aren't the only holiday specials in town. A *Charlie Brown Christmas*, for instance—a favorite of all three of our boys, unfortunately. Setting aside the misogynistic decision to cast venture capitalism as little girls who want nothing more from Santa than cash and real estate, there's a very troubling antienvironmental mythos at work here. Charlie Brown, as you may recall, is encouraged by his friends to buy a "great big aluminum tree" for their Christmas play. Instead of heeding their advice to purchase a reusable, recyclable product, Charlie buys a spindly "real" tree because, and I quote, "I think it needs me."

Viewers might be interested to know there is a term for this, *anthropocentrism*, which some argue is reinforced by certain passages in the Bible. This might be the focus of yet another engaging exercise. What if, for instance, we invite viewers to mute the television when Linus steps on stage to recite the nativity story in Luke, and read aloud instead this quote from Genesis 1:26: "Then God said, 'Let us make humankind in our image, according to our likeness; and let them have dominion over the fish of the sea, and over the birds of the air, and over the cattle, and over all the wild animals of the earth, and over every creeping thing that creeps upon the earth'"?

It might lead a few of them to ask, rightly: "Who's the real creep in this story?"

Speaking of, when Charlie Brown's weakened sapling buckles under the weight of one ornament, he cries a little, then abandons it. If Charles Shultz had been interested in revealing a hard truth about the human relationship to the environment, he might have ended it right there. Instead, here comes spiritual healer Linus to declare "all it needs is a little love." With the help of his friends, Linus decorates the tree with lights and baubles and, in the process, miraculously restores its foliage. It is a well-known fact that once needles fall off deciduous trees, whether from (in Charlie's case) dehydration or (in our case) bagworms, they don't come back.

Hey, Peanuts gang, this isn't a frickin' mulberry!

Again, a children's holiday show like this may seem relatively harmless, but then this happens.... I'm out in the yard yesterday, perusing a small hillside garden where I've unsuccessfully tried to establish prairie plants over the last couple of years. Alden joins me and asks what's up. "I'm sad," I reply, because I don't believe in hiding grown-up emotions from children. "Nothing made it." That's when he literally hits me in the thigh and says, "Maybe you don't *love it enough*."

Seriously?

Love has nothing to do with it, I was tempted to tell him. It has to do with soil type and shade and competing cool season plants, like blue grass and creeping charlie and wild grape vines, which have choked the life out of almost everything I've planted here. It also has to do with the fact that our yard is part of the Loess Hills, which used to be sun-bathed grasslands and oak savannas, but is now largely overrun by woodland plants and housing developments. And deer (pl.), which mowed down more than a few of my young plants. Finally, it has to do with the fact that prairie ecologies are among the most endangered in the world, and those in Iowa the most endangered of all.

Instead, I reminded Alden that daddy has, in fact, written several books on the subject of prairie habitats and appreciation, and that maybe someday soon he'll be forced to read them. That's another kind of love.

But then he reminded me that actually there were flowers growing there in the summer. He was referring, I think, to the wild bergamot, a native prairie plant commonly called "bee balm," which had indeed thrived in that spot and would likely return next summer. Which reminded me that at least one of the little bluestem grass clumps had also survived, its wine-like colors ornamenting the hillside this very autumn.

Which then reminded me, strangely, of an incident involving his older brother, Spencer, when he was about Alden's age. It concerned my own grandmother, with whom I had shared many childhood holiday rituals—tree decorating, making divinity candies (though the walnuts made the roof of my mouth peel), and baking wafer-thin sugar cookies shaped as trees, stars, and, yes, flying reindeer (pl.).

Although Alden never met "Gramma K," as we affectionately called her, I was glad our two oldest were able to experience some of these traditions with her before she died at age ninety-two. Spencer was three at the time and asked a lot of tearful questions, such as: Why did Gramma have to die? Doesn't God love her? Will I ever see her again?

These are real stumpers for a parent, I can assure you. They might even be seen as the foundation of most major religions. Certainly implied was the possibility of a Jesus-like resurrection in this world or the next, but the name Jesus never once crossed Spencer's lips. Instead, one day he just declared: "Maybe Santa will make Gramma K come back, like Frosty."

He was referring, of course, to the Rankin/Bass show!

After Frosty is trapped and melted in that poinsettia greenhouse, devastating his young friend Karen, Santa arrives to restore the snowman to full vigor. Although he must leave for now, Santa assures Karen that Frosty will return every year with the snow. They take off in Santa's sleigh, into the moonlit night, as the song plays in the background: "He'll be back again someday."

I guess from Spencer's perspective, one of the "nice" lessons of this show was that every year the snow returns, and, as promised, snow people sprout up all over the yard. Why not a grandma or two?

Or even a prairie?

When I think about it, maybe young idealists like Alden and Spencer and Linus are correct, that love does have something to do with resurrections of the nature sort. At prairie restorations, I've heard scientists and citizen volunteers use terms like "love" and "faith" alongside more technical terms like "climax communities" and "cotyledon." There are, of course, all kinds of ecological—and yes, Lucy, economic—benefits to prairie restoration, but in the end, for many of these people, it boils down to something like: "We've killed it. It needs a little love."

And thanks to this emotional engagement, along with hard work and accumulating scientific knowledge, there are places near us where prairie ecosystems have made a remarkable, if forever incomplete, comeback.

But don't get a big head, Mr. Roth. I still think it is irresponsible to teach children that all such losses can be magically reversed. As our pet goldfish only recently demonstrated. Even so, it's hard to deny what these same children observe every year: the seasonal return of life from seeming death.

Furthermore—and here's another entertaining research project for kids—at the molecular level, the pieces that made up Frosty or the person my sons knew and loved as Gramma K or the vast wild places of old, have not vanished entirely. They have transformed, entering into a different state of existence. As I've told the children many times, with mixed success, the concept of a self-contained division between body, mind, and environment—imposed on us by religious and secular dogma—is, at that same molecular level, factually inaccurate. We are all connected, blending with one another; physical beings temporarily manifested before dissolving once again into the All-ness.

Such concepts harbor their own risks, I know: imagine if children walked around conscious of the fact that they are breathing their grandparents! Or a prairie or anything or anyone we've ever loved or should have loved that has ever been lost. All of it circling in and out of our bodies, all the time—inhaling to sustain a momentary existence, exhaling into eternal possibilities. What would it lead to?

Maybe faith and resolve.

Maybe insanity.

On a related note, I've heard that some of the original Animagic puppets have survived and are in private hands. I wonder what those people are doing with them and if they'd ever consider selling. They are no doubt worth an arctic gold mine. If auctioned, the money might be used to buy actual Christmas gifts for poor kids living in the modern equivalent of unheated mangers or donated to an environmental organization that protects actual penguins in their actual habitats. Something to make this biosphere a healthier home for real-life creatures, including children.

Still, it's kind of fun imagining what I would offer to purchase those puppets and present them to a future, grown-up Alden and his brothers, taking a little memory-ride together on the Yestermorrowbile. Actually, that would make a great, final bonus question to include in the proposed guide: *What price would you pay to own or otherwise have dominion over these stuffed, embodied metaphors and all they've ever represented to you and those you love?*

I think the answers could be interesting, ranging from nothing to something pretty substantial. Like ten million dollars.

Or the world.

Affectionately yours,
John Price

MY SCIENCE FICTION HORROR STORY

Secret of the Ninth Planet (A Weird Tale)

My brain whirled; and where before I had attempted to explain
  things away,
I now began to believe in the most abnormal and incredible wonders.
—H. P. Lovecraft, *The Whisperer in the Dark*

It is only now, over four years later, in the safety of my study, having lit my pipe and poured a crystalline dram of courage, that I am finally able to set down on paper the story of my amazing journey with a strange being from another world. As you will soon learn, it was alongside this amorphous life form—or "creature," as I was accustomed to calling it—that I found myself, in autumn-tide, unexpectedly traversing the vast, ever-darkening reaches of time and space behind which, as Mr. Lovecraft once observed, there lurk "facts of the most stupendous and vista-opening nature."

It was out there, on the very edge of an incalculable abyss, that this creature and I encountered a lonely and long-hidden planet inhabited by icy secrets that even now tax my feeble gifts of comprehension.

Given the fantastical nature of my adventure and its revelations, you may rightly ask why it is I have waited this long to share it publicly, now that the creature is beyond the reach of scientific dissection.

I can reply only, in shame, that I have acted out of base fear. Not fear of the creature, which has all but vanished from my daily and (what now seems) pathetically circumscribed existence. Rather, that my story, once public, would be met with disbelief and mockery or worse, indifference.

For it is a tale that, in its infinite variety, has been told many times before; so much so, there are those who would believe it common. It is not common.

But where to start? I suppose it all begins and ends with the creature himself, which I'll do my best to introduce here, though aspects of his nature, like that of all living beings, defy verbal articulation. As I have said, I considered him a strange life-form, yet at the time of our journey, he was not unknown to me. We had, in fact, lived in close proximity to one another for twelve years. I had seen him grow and transmogrify numerous times, beginning with the moment when, still in larval stage, he emerged covered in viscous goo from my wife's suddenly foreign body—an oozing, originating biosphere and interstellar channel where scientists postulate his kind briefly manifest salamander tails and finger-webbing and gill slits, breathing not air, but water and (of all the horrors!) their own excrement.

Any wonder their entrance into our world is met with screams?

Be that as it may, the creature, once emerged, immediately exerted a strange and irresistible power over me and my poor, still-bloodied wife. Through emotive telepathy, the tiny, squalling flesh caterpillar (for that is what it most resembled) commanded that we should nurture and protect it for as long as it so desired, even to the point of sacrificing our lives. Some have referred to this power as "love," but that seems a milquetoast word for it, as there was also no small degree of terror, born of a new and potentially crushing responsibility. Regardless, we were instantly under its control. Then began, as I have intimated, a series of dramatic metamorphoses, both mental and physical, that I will not describe here, other than to say they occurred at a speed that beggars imagination.

At the dawn of the journey I am about to describe, the creature was on the verge of its greatest metamorphosis to date, one that would dramatically change its physical and emotional characteristics and, not unlike the Methuselah generation of monarch butterfly, infuse it with startling capabilities—including, heaven forbid, the ability to reproduce!

Temporarily, however, the creature appeared to the rote senses to be a youngish male humanoid of scarcely three meters in height, of lithe build and musculature, throughout which could be discerned a restless, twitchy energy that rendered it incapable of concentrating or remaining still for periods exceeding forty-two-and-one-half seconds. His skin (what little was visible beneath the hooded smock favored by his kind) was a coppery hue from hours spent submerged in various outdoor aquariums—for the species worships both sun and water— and nearly hairless but for the top of his cranium, from which grew an often dirty, fibrous density the color of harvest straw.

Of the creature's ways of communicating, I can say only that there have been many and all equally confounding, but at the time of this adventure, he was partial to random outbursts of gibberish suggesting predilections for trivial earth knowledge and wordplay that he alone deemed entertaining, informative, and/or cleverly insulting. Here is but one example, spoken near the time of our departure.

"Hey, Dad, wanna hear a joke that becomes a paradox? Pinocchio says, 'My nose will grow.'"

Many times, after such a vociferation, I wished for the appropriate Rosetta Stone that I might make sense of its relevancy. Perhaps there is some clue to be found in the title the creature sometimes (but not always) answered to, "Spencer," from the Anglo-French for "dispenser of goods." Indeed, these obscure interjections were *dispensed* with such frequency during our journey I have decided to transcribe them here, without edit or comment, however inconvenient to the narrative (and to my peace of mind), for they seem part and parcel of the nature of the creature himself. Even his term for me, "Dad," so long in use, occasionally retained an unfamiliar ring, as if he were speaking to a being distinct from myself.

The sensation was not unpleasant. I say only that it was, at various times, *weird*.

Taken altogether, then, I considered my companion a remarkable specimen, and in fact he was unique in all the universe, though strangers would not have thought so. Indeed, as we prepared to board the ship—a great shiny bird of a machine!—in the metropolitan port of Omaha, nobody seemed to take notice of the One following me into the cabin. Nor did they suspect that while most of us had ventured forth on similar vessels, this was the creature's first time doing so. We were thus in the presence of a brain more akin to those of a thousand years ago, for whom flight was experienced only in dream or religious ecstasy.

Indeed, as we ascended into the lower atmosphere, a rare stillness came over the creature who, face pressed against the window, observed for the first time the tops of clouds, which he described in awe as "ice cream" and "cotton candy" and "mashed potatoes," reaching, as the primitive imagination will, for the familiar in the face of profundity. That, or the creature was once again hungry. He continued babbling excitedly at mountains and cities, rendered small and insignificant, or rather *newly* significant, while others of my kind idly fiddled with their handheld devices or shut their windows, that they might slumber.

There are those who would diminish such raw openness to new knowledge and experience as the ordinary, even naive manifestations of the "tween" mind—as if a mere bridge between more significant states of mental being, child and adolescent/adult (those inhabited as it so happens by his younger and older siblings), but I no longer believe it so.

Rather, I have come to think that in such a mind—too briefly with us—may be found the salvation of our world.

■

"Hey, Dad, after you order food in a restaurant, don't you literally become *the waiter?*"

This brain-warper was emitted by the creature shortly after voraciously consuming, to my nauseous consternation, a sardine and onion pizza. We were sitting inside a ruinous tavern, in the modest city of learning known as Flagstaff, Arizona, the destination toward which we had flown those thousand miles above the clouds. During the previous two days, I had attended an inspiring gathering of fellow literati, but wasted little time in fleeing it, for I sensed the creature, though well-fed and offered access to a swimming pool and television (enough previously to make him content), was growing dangerously agitated.

"Hey, Dad, what did the cannibal do after dumping her boyfriend? Wiped her butt! *Hah!* Get it?"

Thus it was that we found ourselves arriving that very afternoon at one of the Seven Wonders of the World known, tamely, as "The Grand Canyon." Walking along its upper rim, we gleaned informational signs that described the concept of a solid and stratified time—nearly six million years—which would defy belief, if not in physical evidence all about us. Here again, above a chasm of seemingly immeasurable dimensions, the creature's raw openness of mind was in full conflagration, absorbing into itself one of the true marvels of our planet. Such was the degree of its infectiousness that, though I had visited the canyon before, it was as if I, too, were discovering it for the first time.

I did not, however, fully share in the creature's exhilarations. While descending the South Kaibab trail, I unwisely confessed to him that the various vulnerabilities of my aged body, especially my knees, were only being amplified by his seeming boundless vitality.

"Aw, c'mon Dad, you won't fall down the cliff. But if you do, I'll call you *butter* cuz you'll be *on a roll! Hah!*"

There was no mercy in this response, only impatience, even judgment. And yet it was clear the creature wanted me with him, that he would not move forward without my companionship. Such was the persistent paradox of our relations.

In any case, I soon found myself moving in steep decline along the switchbacks of that precipitous path, through the layers of Kaibab Limestone and Toroweap Formation, beneath the appropriately named "Pustule Dome," where whitish protrusions of Permian-age sediment had emerged from the softer, flesh-like limestone—prescient, perhaps, of the soon-to-be condition of the creature's facial complexion. All about us the Earth opened, mouth-like, into inconceivable depths, and many times I felt some irresistible force, an invisible tentacle maybe, reaching to pull me into the maw. I threw myself back against the towering cliffside that I might edge more slowly past the danger. The creature experienced no such fear, as he frequently, and with enthusiasm, drew himself to the very edge of the breech—a thrill-seeking instinct heretofore unrecognized by those claiming to know his nature.

Nowhere was this more evident than at a terrifying precipice known as "Ooh-Ahh Point." Named such because the first sight of it often evokes involuntary, terror-filled vocalizations. I was no different, for in the moment that near-infinite view of the east canyon opened before my eyes, I sensed in my throat the rise of both sound and bile. The creature, in stark contrast, immediately clambered up a nature-hewn pyramid of boulders, stood erect, and flapped his arms like a pale, featherless bird set to take flight. Sure evidence that this being's exuberance for life had rendered all mortal concerns, including death itself, irrelevant.

Alas, not so for me.

The view of him up there, on the brink of the abyss, was too much to bear. And yet, when I attempted to climb upon the rock and pull the creature to safety, and deliver a well-deserved scolding, my limbs became paralyzed. You may mock, but let me assure you, dear reader, the danger was real—indeed, only a few months later, from the exact spot where the creature now flapped, a misfortunate woman would accidentally topple many hundreds of feet to an untimely death. Even so, to my eternal shame, I could not bring myself to approach him, though I did shout—*was it a scream?*—that he should promptly un-perch. Mercifully, he obeyed, but not without comment.

"Geez, you're just like Carolyn's dad. He leaves the porch light on all the time because someone said there was a mountain lion in the neighborhood. I told her to call him 'scare-*dee*-cat'!"

That night, through the pitch-dark desert, we rode back to Flag-staff. The place we had just explored was indeed a wonder of the world, and I was filled to the brim by it, exhausted, but I sensed the creature was as yet unsatisfied. I do not wish to diminish the sublime immensity of that legendary rift, but I have come to believe its scope, however awe-inspiring, was no match for the scope of this creature's growing cravings of intellect and imagination. The canyon, however grand, was too earth-bound, too much about the past—already known and claimed by countless others of my kind.

In the eerie light of the dashboard, the creature's silent expression seemed to ask: *Is there not something more? Something my own?*

Indeed, the discovery of his true planetary abode was yet before us.

■

"Hey, Dad, did you know studies say it takes literally two months to break a bad habit? So, like, could you at least wait that long before scolding me again about wiping my hands on my shorts? I'd *definitely* appreciate it."

This impudent perturbation occurred in the car the next morning, following a late and chaotic lunch of yet another stomach-churning pizza. With some effort, I resisted responding and soon we were on our way to that hour's destination: the Lowell Observatory.

Why there? you ask—as did I when first the creature chose it, just hours earlier. I had been reading from a brochure of possible desti-nations for that day, and at the mention of interplanetary discover-ies, he suddenly bolted upright from his hotel bed-nest. *There!* he commanded. I thought he might have chosen instead a water park, but something deep within must have already felt the place calling, drawing us closer to its dark revelations. Even then, I felt some vague foreboding, which I dismissed as concern that such an "educational" place might, as in the past, be a disappointment to him. If so, his silent sulking would assuredly transform the minutes into lifetimes.

"Hey, Dad, did you hear about the zoo where the only animal they had was a dog? It was a *shih tzu!* Get it?"

But it was too late for regret, our path was set.

The observatory was but on the other side of this modest human settlement, yet seemingly worlds away, set at the top of a geographic elevation known as "Mars Hill"—for reasons soon to be revealed. The moment our vehicle entered the grounds, it was engulfed by a dense mist, and still we climbed higher, carefully navigating the twisted road through an ever-entangling forest of towering pines, ghost-white aspens, and shadowy, tentacled oaks.

"Hey, Dad, do you think this place will have a mechanical claw machine? There's this kid so good at them he's been banned from, like, *every* Walmart in the world. *Seriously.*"

At last, we arrived at the so-called parking lot, though it was in truth a launching pad to worlds unknown. Before us, half-buried in the earth, was the angular, metal structure known as the Steele Visitor Center. We were greeted inside by a friendly woman who reluctantly divulged that the last tour had already departed. If we hurried, she said, we might intercept the group. As we ran through the rain, heavier now, my lungs sensed for the first time the reality that we were at 7,246 feet above sea level, bringing upon me a spark-blighted dizziness. The creature, far ahead, called back from his ageless Elysium.

"Don't give up, Dad! Think about it this way: you're not fifty years old, just twenty with thirty years of experience!"

I at last caught up to him inside the entrance to the Slipher Building and Rotunda Library, relieved to discover our fellow travelers listening to the speech of an elderly guide (perhaps forty with thirty-five years of experience). And what a speech! It was in this very place, the man declared with crust, that the mystery of the expanding universe had been revealed to all humanity. There followed the bracing tale of Vesto Slipher, who on September 17, 1912, using the telescope here at Lowell Observatory, "obtained the first radial velocity of a 'spiral nebula'"—the Andromeda Galaxy!—and eventually established "that large velocities, usually in recession, are a general property of the spiral nebulae."

Though Professor Slipher never received proper recognition or reward (Hubble received most of the glory), his calculations helped prove that the tottering, abysmal edge of the universe is racing away from us, creating horizons that outrun our capacity to reach them, until, on their inevitable return, they find us and create something wholly new. An undulating, galactic metamorphosis of unimaginable proportions.

"Hey, Dad, what if the light we see when we die is us being born out of another woman's vagina? *Whoa*, check out that lamp!"

The creature was whispering loudly and pointing at a large, ornate ceiling lamp in the shape of the planet Saturn. This gaseous goliath was named for the King of the Titans, who devoured his children out of fear and jealousy, only to be tricked by his wife, Ops (goddess of wealth and abundance), and his remaining son, Jupiter, into regurgitating them whole and alive. They promptly imprisoned the Titan ruler for eternity. Saturn was the creature's favorite planet to date, perhaps because of the rings, always striking, or maybe its originating story of a father duped by his children and their mother, that they might supplant him.

"Hey, Dad, check out that giant space shuttle tire over there—it's bald, just like the tires on your Subaru and the *top of your head! Hah!*"

We were soon directed to exit the library, arriving shortly thereafter at the understated, yet epochal, lair of the legendary space instrument known as ... the Clarke Refractor. Inside the structure's dim interior, which resembled a round, wood-planked barn loft, better suited it would seem for milk cows, the copper-sheened telescope towered both above and below us—thirty-two feet long, twenty-four inches in diameter, weighing six tons. Anchored here by Percival Lowell in 1896, the device still pointed heavenward through a slit in the massive dome, its eldritch eye fixed on some distant wonder, while below, at its base, was a simple oak desk with chair. There arrived a shiver of mental revolution as I considered that, from perhaps that very desk, Slipher made his configurations of the expanding universe. Decades later, that same telescopic eye was used to create a detailed map of the surface of the moon for the now-mythic Apollo missions—our first step upon distant and half-darkened worlds.

"Hey, Dad, here's a stumper: Can your left arm be considered a parasite?"

What truly stirred loose in me a subconscious residuum, however, was knowledge that it was through this same telescope that Professor Lowell observed what he thought were *canals* on the surface of Mars. Lowell postulated that these linear, intersecting channels were constructed by an advanced Martian civilization that they might draw precious water from the polar ice caps. The esteemed professor birthed three massive tomes on the subject—*Mars* (1895), *Mars and Its Canals* (1906), and *Mars as the Abode of Life* (1908)—and went to his grave, in 1916, believing his theories to be true. Earlier, in the Rotunda Library, we had perused Lowell's initial photographs, sketchings, and maps of the canals, including Thoth (learning), Amenthes (dream), and Morpheos (death)—names inspired, perhaps, by such other awe-tinctured journeys into the unknown.

That these canals were proven to be but optical illusions concerns only the fleshly quadrants of our mammalian brain. Within that same brain's more expansive, phantasmal regions, Professor Lowell's theory launched our collective being toward heretofore-untold realms of imagination, returning with a wealth of stories and art that confronted, with unprecedented vigor, certain existential truths and possibilities and questions that are as vital now as they were then. Among the most fundamental being: *Are we alone?*

"Hey, Dad, ever since I watched that movie *Psycho* at Colin's house, I'm always looking for peepholes in bathrooms. Is that paranoid?"

I include my own brain among those so elevated by Lowell's "false" discovery. Mars was, in fact, the first interplanetary abode of my young imagination and one that, as for all who gravitate toward distant worlds, revealed something essential to the self, about the self.

It began in the dusty library of Duncombe Elementary School in Fort Dodge, Iowa, when I was but a smidge younger than the creature chirping nonsense beside me. One afternoon, before departing for home, I pulled from the shelves there an intriguing, crimson-covered volume and read this passage:

> In the stone galleries the people were gathered in clusters and groups filtering up into the shadows among the blue hills. A soft evening light shone over them from the stars and the luminous double moons of Mars. Beyond the marble amphitheater, in darkness and distances, lay little towns and villas; pools of silver water stood motionless and canals glittered from horizon to horizon. It was an evening in summer upon the placid and temperate planet Mars. Up and down green wine canals, boats as delicate as bronze flowers drifted. In the long and endless dwellings that curved like tranquil snakes across the hills, lovers lay idly whispering in cool night beds. The last children ran in torchlit alleys, gold spiders in their hands throwing out films of web…. In the amphitheaters of a hundred towns on the night side of Mars the brown Martian people with gold coin eyes were leisurely met to fix their attention upon stages where musicians made a serene music flow up like blossom scent on the still air.

This mesmerizing scene, as you may be aware, was created by the genius Ray Bradbury, and from the moment I entered it, I was lost. I devoured the rest of his *Martian Chronicles* under the covers, at night, the actual planet itself shining down through my open window, before entering my dreams. One minute I was a boy in his bed, in Iowa, and the next I was drifting in boats upon tranquil canals, along fossil seas under twin Martian moons, in a golden civilization where books are played like harps, and crystal houses turn to follow the sun like flowers, and the lavender evenings fill rooms "like a dark wine poured to the ceiling."

It was, indeed, the closest I had come, at that tender age, to intoxication.

"Hey, Dad, speaking of the Red Planet, what's red and smells like blue paint? *Red paint! Get it?*"

But beginning with that phrase "the last children," there also entered into those dreams, as well my waking mind, a new awareness of the destructive bent of human inclinations. There was, to begin with, the near complete obliteration of the native Martians and their children, the last, by way of a disease spread by the first explorers from Earth: chicken pox. A child's disease I had recently suffered myself. In attempting to defend themselves, the Martians used telepathy to delude early astronauts into thinking they had landed among their childhood families and hometowns—including in Iowa!—thus luring them to painless deaths. It caused me to ponder: Could the placid surface of my own hometown also be a dangerous illusion?

What followed in the book was a haunting of endings. Most of all, the ending of Earth itself, scorched by environmental disaster and nuclear war, from which my classmates and I—perhaps the last children on our planet—hid every week beneath our wooden desks.

The next year, in seventh grade, I transported to junior high, where I experienced attendant changes to my body and social status not dissimilar to those I feared were about to engulf my innocent companion—he was already experiencing what was termed by his kind as "bullying." I knew it all too well. During that horrifying metamorphosis, Mars was still my guiding planet, but this time the red orb was ruled by Edgar Rice Burrough's John Carter, a place less about disturbed ponderings of earthly reality, than a merciful escape from them. The adventure begins when Carter, an emotionally scarred Civil

War veteran, is magically transported to the Red Planet, known by the natives as Barsoom, where he becomes a global superhero and weds a princess.

How many times, cowering at my locker from the latest physical threat or public humiliation, had I begged the universe to do the same for me?

"Hey, Dad, true fact: Did you know that more people die each year from coconuts falling on their head than shark attacks?"

I devoured each of the eleven tomes in the John Carter saga, before traveling on to Arrakis/Dune and Tatooine and other strange worlds, including the strangest of all, Adulthood. But I would never fully escape the gravitational pull of Bradbury's Mars, so in sync with the ongoing rhythms of my mind—the lingering sense that, due to the cruelty and arrogance of humanity, there would always be some dreadfulness waiting on the horizon of tomorrow, like the volatile weather of an Iowa summer:

> It was like those days when you heard a thunderstorm coming and there was the waiting silence and then the faintest pressure of the atmosphere as the climate blew over the land in shifts and shadows and vapors. And the change pressed at your ears and you were suspended in the waiting time of the coming storm. You began to tremble. The sky was stained and colored: the clouds were thickened; the mountains took on an iron taint. The caged flowers blew with faint sighs of warning. You felt your hair stir softly. Somewhere in the house the voice clock sang, "Time, time, time, time..." ever so gently, no more than water tapping on velvet.

I thought I heard again that ominous refrain—*time, time, time*—as I witnessed the creature take his turn standing at the base of this mighty telescope, as if to peer into the black eternity of space, seeking new worlds and answers, new selves. Alternative futures.

In contrast, I found myself irresistibly falling into the past, recalling earlier manifestations in which he and I walked, hand in hand, through other realms of discovery. His early love of insects, for instance, and those crustacean marvels called roly-polies that he relentlessly sought beneath rocks, half-naked and wearing red boots after a dousing rain. Or an epic journey our family made to Memphis, Tennessee, named for the Egyptian City of Kings, when he was but five, that we might encounter a living panda, his favorite animal and guiding spirit, which had inspired him to worship all things Chinese. This included an Asian curiosity shop in our local mall, long since closed, where the kind proprietor allowed the younger, smaller manifestation of this creature to water his bamboo plants.

There, I once purchased for him an ornately painted lantern that he might hang it above his tiny head in dream, only to wake again in our arms.

■

"Hey, Dad, you know how Mom complains about her back when she's having her period? I told her she should feel lucky it isn't a *semicolon*. Hah!"

It occurred to me, as we once again walked through the rain, that such ill-advised statements made whatever future this creature imagined for himself highly tenuous. In retrospect, though, I believe he meant to encourage me with levity, as my progress back to the Steele Visitor Center was significantly slowed by knee pain—a lingering consequence of the previous day's trek. Once safely inside its doors, I assumed we would soon depart for the comforts of the hotel. But as fate would have it, a voice from on high announced that later that evening the "Pluto Observatory" would be open for viewing—the very place where the ninth planet had been discovered!

I instantly detected a re-perking of the creature's proclivity, though I explained to him that to stay would mean delaying dinner—perhaps another pizza, however foul. He at once rejected the offer, citing in ever-strengthening terms his desire to see this final station, set at the far reaches of intimate space.

"Hey, Dad, stop *Russian* me—I ain't *Stalin*, I'm just *Putin* a little thought into it!"

There was no choice—I was ever his captive.

To pass the time, we attended (along with perhaps six others) a series of educational lectures that, though I did not think it possible, set the creature's vociferations into even higher gear. The first was by an aging professor on sunspots ("You know how Grandpa always says we're burning daylight? Well, isn't it already being burned—*by the sun?!*") followed by a young university student who demonstrated the effects of frozen nitrogen on balloons ("Did you hear about the kid who lit a fart with a match and blew off both his butt cheeks?") and unleashing the lightning-like plasmatic strings of what she called a "Van de Graaff generator." At her invitation, the creature actually touched the energy streams, causing his hair to stand on end in frightening fashion ("What's the matter, Dad, do I look *shocking?*").

"You know, I conducted a scientific experiment just last week," he informed our young teacher as we departed. "If you plug your nose, raw onions and apple slices taste the same. Seriously, try it sometime."

A sudden change came over him, however, when we entered the artifact room dedicated to the discovery of Pluto. The creature moved more slowly now, from display to display, silently reading the words that, together, created the story of the search for this distant and elusive world.

It began when Professor Lowell momentarily shifted his gaze from the canals of Mars to the planet Neptune, a gaseous giant of immense dimensions, with three minion moons and (as would be revealed later) rings of ancient debris from stellar collisions now lost to time. Any wonder scientists assumed Neptune exerted power over its planetary neighbor, Uranus, named for so-called Father Sky, husband of Gaia, Mother Earth? Uranus is also a gaseous giant, but not equal to Neptune, as evidenced by its warped orbit, which Lowell's contemporaries believed to be the gravitational spell of its oceanic master. Professor Lowell, however, in the long nights at his oaken desk beneath the

Clarke telescope, postulated the behavior of Uranus could not be explained by proximity to Neptune alone, but that another, hidden world must be wielding invisible influence.

A trans-Neptunian presence he deemed "Planet X."

So it was, in 1905, Percival Lowell began the interstellar search that would consume the final years of his life. In his obsession—some called it *madness*—he built or borrowed ever-more powerful telescopes, desperately searching the stars for the mysterious world that haunted his waking dreams. His quest would end unfulfilled in 1916, upon his death.

For over a decade, in the dark of Lowell's stone mausoleum, located but a stick's throw from where we stood, the search for Planet X moldered—a tall tale for the next generation of astronomers to share on autumnal evenings, beneath cold stars. Did any of them sense, in those moments, a strange presence, waiting, calling out from the frozen recesses of space that it might finally be known and worshipped? Regardless, something must have spoken directly, and with irresistible force, into the mind of Professor Lowell's protégé, Vesto Slipher, he of the expanding universe, for the man suddenly took up the lost mission in 1928. Aided by the treasure hordes of Percival's grieving brother, Abbot, Professor Slipher built a mighty device that would take them, and all our kind, where none had gone before

It was christened the Abbot Lawrence Lowell Telescope, and around it they built a separate observatory on Mars Hill. But who would Vesto Slipher call forth to help run this magnificent machine and analyze the troves of data it was poised to collect—breadcrumbs on the trail of a world that might not even exist? Only the most unlikely of interplanetary adventurers, a young Kansas farmer and stargazer turned astronomer, Clyde Tombaugh.

Clyde's youthful drawings of Jupiter and Mars, viewed from a homemade telescope (the components of which, I would note, his father labored a second job to purchase for him) mounted on spare parts collected from a cream operator and the crankshaft of a 1910

Buick, caught the attention of Professor Slipher. He must have seen in them an unusual capacity of mind and imagination (dare I say, *openness?*), for he hired Clyde—at twenty-two, a mere decade older than the creature beside me—to wield the thirteen-inch triple-lens astrograph, birthing photographic plates of select corners of the night sky. In one hour alone, this magnificent machine could capture the images of three hundred thousand stars, which Clyde Tombaugh and his minions scoured for the slightest hint of unfamiliar movement.

Professor Slipher's faith in this remarkable young man did not go unrewarded—had it been preordained?—for on February 18, 1930, Clyde somehow spotted, in that stellar immensity, a small dot that could not be a remnant emulsion on the plate or a speck of dust, for it moved in relation to a particular guide star, Delta Gem. It *moved!* One of the two discovery plates (its twin kept at the Smithsonian Museum in our nation's capital city) was displayed behind glass before which the creature and I now stood, an arrow pointing to that small, yet vista-shattering dot. There, too, was the plate envelope, on which Clyde wrote copious notes, ending with this momentous scribble: "Planet X at last found!!!"

"Hey, Dad, you know how people thought Planet X was a prank? Here's another one. Call someone on the phone and say, 'If a cow laughs, does milk come out of its nose?' *Then hang up!*"

It was with much relief that I greeted the announcement that the Pluto Observatory was at last open. I anticipated a crush of fellow human beings, all clamoring to visit this legendary site, but we emerged from the side room to discover we were alone. We made our way slowly up the rain-dampened path to the telescope—the skies had cleared, and the sun nearly fallen beneath the horizon, enfolding Mars Hill in growing shadow. The effect provoked in me an ominous feeling, amplified by the presence of the planets themselves, as pictured on informative signs placed in proper order along the trail. It was as if we were traversing the length of the solar system itself—more than four billion miles!

As we journeyed outward from the sun, each planet brought to me intimate, even sentimental associations, drawn from the literature and myths and wisdom of my generation and before. The winged shoes of Mercury, delivering flowers; clouded Venus, where a schoolgirl was cruelly locked in a closet by bullies, missing summer's only sunny day; home Earth, where the Statue of Liberty waited to be buried waist-deep in war-irradiated sands; then Mars (my very own) and Jupiter, King of Planets, bringer of jollity and the regal strains of Holst's symphonic worship; Saturn, whose ringed visage served as the template for countless planetary representations; Neptune, long-bearded and raising his mighty trident on a billboard above the city of San Diego, where first I saw the ocean as a boy, as wondrous to me then as the entirety of space. Then the eighth planet, enshrouded by reclusive densities, devoid of personal associations, if only for a blessed moment.

"Hey, Dad, if I launch a rocket at your butt, isn't it technically landing on Ur-*anus*? *Hah!*"

Finally, we approached the sign dedicated to Pluto. While the other planets had long thrived in the collective imagination of my species, Pluto seemed, by comparison, an empty place. How had the human mind populated this obscure orb, if at all?

At first, I could find no answer, but then, from the outer reaches of memory, I retrieved a story encountered during my own adolescence, titled "The Whisperer in the Dark." It was written by Mr. H. P. Lovecraft, whose grotesque imaginings would haunt me on many a night that followed. Published in 1930, shortly after the discovery of the ninth planet, Lovecraft might have been first among literary mind-travelers to visit its frigid surface.

And what did he find there? A place of terrors beyond imagining. A bleak realm that "ought to be enough to make any man a Dante or Poe if he can keep sane long enough to tell what he has seen." This was not a temperate paradise of green wine rivers and lavender evenings, where an elegant civilization sang the music of books. No, the cities of this world were instead enshrouded by impermeable darkness, "great tiers of terraced towers built of black stone" where "black rivers of pitch" flowed under "mysterious Cyclopean bridges."

In the story, this hope-blighted description was voiced by the "whisperer in the dark," disguised by perverse means as a human citizen of Vermont. He was, in truth, among the malevolent "Outer Ones" inhabiting this nightmarish planet, "members of a cosmos-wide race of which all other life-forms are merely degenerate variants," and who intend to colonize Earth. The Outer Ones are, he claims, "more vegetable than animal," a combination of fungoid structure and a kind of chlorophyll-like substance, perhaps what scientists on Earth would deem "lichenized." Indeed, the earth lichen called "sunburst" has traveled on silver ships into the wastes of space and returned in full vigor, just as an Outer Being "is unique in its ability to traverse the heatless and airless interstellar void in full corporeal form." The Whisperer continues with this now haunting prophecy:

> Their main immediate abode is a still undiscovered and almost lightless planet at the very edge of our solar system—beyond Neptune, and the ninth in distance from the sun. It is, as we have inferred, the object mystically hinted at as "Yuggoth" in certain ancient and forbidden writings; and it will soon be the scene of a strange focusing of thought upon our world in an effort to facilitate mental rapport. I would not be surprised if astronomers became sufficiently sensitive to these thought-currents to discover Yuggoth when the Outer Ones wish them to do so.... Don't tell anyone about it, of course—for this matter must not get to the promiscuous public.

Beyond Mr. Lovecraft, however, literary flights to this newly discovered world could hardly be described as promiscuous. Nothing close to those inspired by Professor Lowell's Martian canals. Perhaps because there were seemingly more pressing considerations for American citizenry in the 1930s, including a catastrophic economic collapse and the approaching specter of yet another world war.

Still, as my research would later reveal, the literature of Pluto was not beyond addressing such Earthly concerns. Stanton A. Colbentz, in his unnerving account of 1931, *Into Plutonian Depths*, describes the first human journey to this distant world. There, beneath the icy surface, the travelers discover a realm "of unimaginable weirdness and beauty" populated by the "Lamp-Heads"—slender, humanoid-like creatures, some of them seven feet tall, each with a "phosphorescent orb" growing out of their craniums—like those of "deep sea fishes!" Plutonian society is cruelly divided into castes: male, female, and neuter. The latter, as the ruling order, greedily horde treasure and enslave those they deem inferior, disseminating their propaganda in a newspaper entitled the *Daily Neuter*, whose motto is: "A helping hand pays no dividend."

Such was the thinking of many an earthling at the time, and even now.

"*Hello?* Earth to Dad? I asked you a question. Why does a flamingo stand on one leg? Because he would *fall over! Duh!*"

Currently, the creature was himself standing on one leg, his parasitical left arm propped on the shoulders of a nearby bronze of Clyde Tombaugh—the very man who, according to Mr. Lovecraft's imaginings, was the target of alien fungoid telepathy, hastening our collective destruction. The creature beside me, however, treated the great astronomer as if he were just another schoolyard peer.

And in their infinite curiosity of mind, weren't they?

Tombaugh, who died in 1997, would not live to see the first close-up satellite images of the world he discovered. One of those images, among the most recent, was displayed on the sign before us, presenting a brownish sphere with unusual dark and light swirling. Beneath it, a placard stated that from the beginning of its discovery in 1930, astronomers considered Pluto "an unusual planet"—or perhaps not a planet at all. This description seemed to spark a visceral reaction in my companion, who had been deemed, at times, "unusual" by his peers.

In a gesture of perhaps growing solidarity, the creature requested that I take a picture of him next to the image, in which it appeared (a clever optical illusion) that he was holding Pluto entirely in his hand. As I did so, there seemed something familiar lurking in the orb's surface markings, some secret meaning I could not place my finger on. The creature then stuck his own finger up Clyde's nose.

"Hey, Dad, here's another scientific fact. Did you know it's actually healthy to eat your boogers? They're *loaded* with good bacteria."

I soon forgot about the picture as we continued past a sign describing the Outer Solar System—a mysterious sweep of numerous solar bodies known as the Kuiper Belt (which includes Pluto) and the Oort Cloud, an ever-widening gateway into the infinite unknown. We at last arrived at the Pluto Observatory, where a placard declared it the official "Discovery site of the ninth planet of the solar system." Yet it was a modest structure, two stories and round, resembling a medieval watchtower made of stones. It was capped with what appeared an angular dome of oaken boards, slatted and painted white, though its sheen revealed them to be metal.

We stepped through the doorway and discovered we were once again alone, surrounded by a silence that would rival any temple during evening vespers. The creature was impatient to ascend to the second floor, that he might gaze upon the mighty instrument of discovery for which the building was named, but I felt a vague dread. I delayed, insisting we visit the various displays, that we might arm ourselves first with knowledge.

The nearest described the naming of the new planet. In Mr. Lovecraft's tale, the narrator states that it was astronomers who, "with a hideous appropriateness they little suspect," named it after the Roman god of the underworld. In fact, it was a tween around the age of my companion. As the story goes, following the announcement of the discovery in March 1930, there was a flood of letters and telegrams suggesting names for this new planetary neighbor. These included Perseus, Vulcan, and Minerva, the goddess of wisdom—originally the front runner, but the name had already been granted to an asteroid. Percival Lowell's widow suggested naming it after herself, "Constance," while

Cronos was the favorite of Lowell's trustee, Roger Lowell Putnam, who, like the aging Mrs. Lowell, heard with more frequency that fearful refrain: *Time, Time, Time....*

The name Pluto was, in contrast, nominated by an eleven-year-old girl from England, Venitia Burney, who read and loved the old Greco-Roman myths—as I had as a boy—and for whom time and death were, as with the creature beside me, mere fictions. Initially, the name was rejected because it might be associated with a popular laxative at the time, called "Pluto Water," granting unwelcome prescience to Lovecraft's imagined "black rivers of pitch." In the end, however, Putnam and the rest "conceded that Pluto's two brothers Jupiter and Neptune already had a place in the solar system and it was time for Pluto to join them."

As for Venitia, Cronos proved forgiving, as she lived to be ninety.

"Hold on, was Pluto a middle kid?"

I couldn't tell the creature the exact birth order of the gods, but it hardly mattered. He was already laying claim to the planet, just as Venitia had, for his own kind.

Before my very eyes, there emerged among the various displays a story dramatically different in tone from those in the data-obsessed visitor's center or the science fiction stories fed by adult phobias, prejudices, and lusts. In a Philadelphia newspaper, for instance, dated March 16, 1930, a cartoon depicted a stork delivering a baby, labeled "The newly discovered planet," to the family of planets, all boys, except for Venus in pigtails. In another cartoon from the *Cleveland News*, Papa Sun, who is bald and dressed in a business suit, smoking a cigar, beams proudly as his planetary colleagues admire baby Pluto.

Here was a planet represented as a child!

There was even a collection of children's books focused on Pluto, displayed alongside a plush gray orb sporting kind eyes and a smile. I could tell the creature strongly coveted this stuffed toy (sold out, regrettably), though he seemed self-conscious in the asking, which brought upon me a sudden sadness. Since he was but a newly emerged larva, he had adored "snuggle buddies," as he called them, gathering to himself a cuddly ecosystem that included such endangered Earth creatures as a giant panda, a sea turtle, a rhino, a red-headed woodpecker, and a Sasquatch. My wife and I had a picture of him alongside his hero, celebrated naturalist Jane Goodall, each holding their respective snuggle buddies—she carried a toy monkey everywhere she spoke, the gift of a blind friend. In elementary school, this creature had been among the first to join Dr. Goodall's local Roots & Shoots program, a transglobal educational force, which inspired him and his peers to plant a native prairie garden beside the playground.

A small beautification of this world, in defiance of those (like me) too often bereft of hope.

"Hey, Dad, did you know that Pluto had a three-headed dog guarding the realm of the dead? Wouldn't it be cool if the Disney Pluto had three heads and was a zombie? No bully would mess with him then!"

Pluto might itself be considered threatened, at least the manner in which it has long been envisaged by its worshippers. The trouble began—as it had for certain unusual individuals entering middle school—when, in 2005, Pluto forcibly entered a "new school" of orbiting objects, previously unknown. First came the discovery of Eris (named for the Greek goddess of strife and discord), which is slightly larger than Pluto, and which temporarily claimed a position as the tenth planet, receiving little fanfare. Then came the discovery of smaller minions, Haumea (Hawaiian goddess of childbirth) and Makemake (Rapa Nui god of fertility, code named "Easter Bunny"), also encircling the sun within the Kuiper Belt.

Together these newly discovered orbs formed an unholy alliance that disseminated confusion and discord among scientists. For as is the tendency of all adult-kind, these astronomers had earlier invented a system of classification from which they were now reluctant to depart. According to this system, a "planet" must be in orbit around the sun, be nearly round in shape, and must have "the gravitational muscle to sweep up or scatter objects near their orbit." It was upon this last point that Pluto was judged insufficient, and thus reclassified as a "dwarf planet."

"First of all, Dad, the word 'dwarf' is *very* offensive—it should be *little* planet!"

Indeed, the new designation of Pluto was offensive to countless numbers worldwide, who protested what they saw as an unearned demotion. The International Astronomical Union attempted to assuage public outrage, recognizing "Pluto's special place in our solar system by designating dwarf planets that orbit the sun beyond Neptune as plutoids." Although admirable, I felt this attempt did not adequately recognize that the issue was, for many, more personal, as evidenced by the editorial cartoons being intensely studied by the creature. I list them here, that readers might make their own inferences:

- Planet Pluto pictured on a street corner, holding a can and a sign: "Victim of Downsizing"

- Planet Pluto pictured as a little boy with baseball bat standing forlornly beneath a tree house, on which is painted: "Solar System Club: Planets Only." From its doorway, a voice shouts: "Beat it, Pluto—you little ice ball!"

- Pluto pictured sitting at a miniature table with other small orbs, while Earth and the other established planets sit at large formal table nearby. Pluto is thinking: *I can't believe I have to sit at the "Little Planets" table.*

- Under a header that reads "Guest Planet Program," all the planets are pictured in their orbits, with Earth declaring, "If Pluto wants to be a citizen of the Solar System, it better straighten out its orbit and act like the rest of us!"

Missing was any acknowledgment of Pluto's starring role in the aforementioned science fiction literature. Yet there was enough here before our eyes to prove that Pluto, along with Mars and the rest of the planets, had been the focus of global-sized admiration and awe, of unapologetic identification.

I pondered: *Might that too be a system by which to classify a planet?*

In this regard, no Eris or Makemake or, god forbid, Ceres—a mere asteroid yet similarly classified a dwarf planet, an equal—could approach its regal drapery. Should the fact that Pluto did not have enough gravitational force to clear an orbital path through space be all that matters? Should it not also matter that it had done the same through the detritus of real-life human sufferings and aspirations, lifting weary eyes once again to the heavens to think, to wonder, to reflect back upon ourselves? Pluto had been born into our collective imagination as a planet, lore had grown up around it—the sacred accumulation of story, myth, metaphor, and sentiment! Before this greater force, all arbitrary, perpetually cold scientific classifications of planets should bow low, as it would outlive such labels for as long as humanity survived.

"Hey, Dad, you know what I said when this bully at school called me 'special ed'? I told him, 'I'm definitely special, but I don't know who Ed is!' That shut him up, *real quick.*"

It was clear from this latest oral emulsion that yet another personal story was approaching orbit around the ninth planet, heated by righteous and empathetic outrage, born of a similarly overlooked sibling, the underdog, the unusual. The One who has watched an older sibling clear his orbit of defensive tackles while running for touchdowns and fame. The One who has at times expressed, in his own verbal bizarrie, mystification at being stranded on a green-diminishing planet that does not fully accept nor nurture the idealistic nature of his kind. Endangering the very openness of mind I spoke of earlier, likewise open to the pain of all creation, and its belief that such pain can ultimately be alleviated—through mere kindness, conviction, laughter.

On the verge of this new metamorphosis, did he suspect the inevitable waning of this openness within himself? Did he see in me and other adult-kind, his own future, a cynical, fearful destination to which he did not wish to venture?

That he might find another way was at once my greatest fear and my greatest hope.

■

And so it was that we finally ascended the winding stairway, toward the machine that in history first birthed the cosmic linkage between our world and the ninth planet. As we did so, the creature surprised me by taking my hand.

"Hey, Dad, sorry about the bald joke earlier. You should think of it this way: your head isn't bald, it's just a solar panel for a writing god. *Hah!* You know I love ya."

He released his grip and continued upward. It was a brief moment, consistent with this being's idiosyncrasies to date. Yet in retrospect, I believe it to be a coded message or injunction, a final gift even, that I might remember and write down what was about to occur. For it would surpass all previous trepidations.

The space was dim, bathed in strange orange glowing, through which I perceived a distinct and vast atmospheric tensity. When my eyes adjusted, the full scope of the wood-planked dome revealed itself. It was half the size of the Lowell Observatory, yet felt more immense. Suddenly, as if called forth from the shadows by our wonderment, there appeared the figure of a young woman—perhaps twelve, with ten years of experience—who stepped toward us and invited all questions. The creature's brain pounced, gathering data with a ferocious urgency I had hardly witnessed before: *How big is Pluto?* (1,393 miles in diameter); *How far away is it from the sun?* (3.67 billion miles); *How many moons does it have?* (three, including Charon, discovered in 1977); *How many days is a year on Pluto?* (90,400). *How long would it take someone to travel there from Earth?*

It was this last question that sent a prophetic shiver up my spine.

"It depends on the means of transportation," responded the Whisperer in the Dark. "The New Horizon space craft took nine years to get there and is this very minute gathering photos and information. But there are faster ways."

And with that, she introduced us to the great telescope before us. It might, at first glimpse, be described as a large metal tube. Though not quite as long as the Clarke telescope, its girth was more substantial, imparting, along with its flesh-like coloration, the illusion of musculature, as if hewn from the shoulder of a Titan. It was indeed attached to a steel-girded, trestle-like arm extending into the upper reaches of the dome. Two mighty axles allowed the massive device to be moved along north-to-south/east-to-west trajectories. In a clownish gesture noticeably appreciated by the creature, someone had stuck a boxing glove on the end of a protruding grip rod, that no one might lose their head, until the proper time.

It was then that my companion moved suddenly forward and boldly gripped the handles of the telescope. Sensing imminent, perhaps expensive catastrophe, I lunged as if to restrain him, but the Whisperer assured me it was OK, that he was welcome to move the mighty machine. Which he did, slowly, back and forth, while robotically chanting:

"I. Am. Stephen. Hawking."

"He's a cute one," remarked the Whisperer.

The creature abruptly stopped his movements, and the huge telescope went still. He turned and asked—in a lowered voice that was not Dr. Hawking's, yet just as unfamiliar, a sure sign his metamorphosis was perilously close—where he might look to see the planet Pluto. She reminded us that the telescope did not contain the usual eyepieces and spectrographs found on other telescopes. It is, instead, an astrographic camera, whose triple lenses feast on a small portion of the night sky, transferring the data onto a photographic plate.

"However," she added, "the long metal tube attached to the underside is an actual telescope. It can be used to locate the star or planet you want to visit."

"Like Pluto?" the creature asked.

"Yes," the Whisperer responded.

The creature looked back at me one last time, smiled, then placed his eye against the scope.

It was but a small gesture, yet there went through me an electric current of fright, nay terror—*what was happening should be stopped, must be stopped!*

But, no—as at Ooh-Ahh Point, I became paralyzed, as if a strangling telepathy had been imposed on me by the Whisperer or by Beings from the Outer Rim of the Solar System, where this creature was now directing all his mental energies! In terms of what he could actually see, there was nothing—the roof of the dome was closed to the night sky. And yet for all that, I knew what appeared in his mind's eye, for I could see it too. There was before him the swirlings of a strange brownish planet that, despite being named for the dread Lord of Death, was no match for the leveling mind powers of this creature. In the beam of his irrepressible gaze, his insatiable, fearless curiosity and longing and quirkiness—his beautiful, weird soul—it was being drawn ever nearer.

Within reach, even!

And then, before my very mind, they became one, the creature and the planet, perched on the edge of the unknown, around which people and memories, like moons, momentarily fell into orbit. Including roly-polies and a thousand furry toy animals and a living panda and all the storefront bamboo plants that had ever thirsted and been given water by his hand. Including, also, the visceral memory of the touch of that same hand, on the steps ascending to this moment, but also as he took his first steps on this planet and across countless playgrounds and parking lots and beneath a million trees, holding the first green crayon he ever used to capture images from the infinite universe of his imagination. Including, finally, the child-self of this being whom I loved, now moving out and away from me, as if already at the other end of the telescope, venturing into reaches unknown—*Time, Time, Time....*

I was then suddenly alone, adrift in a strange and ever-darkening orbit. Instinctively, I reached out for him, but it was too late.

He was gone.

This was the great secret of Pluto, I thought. *The haunting of endings.* And then I thought no more.

∎

These four years later, I have little memory of events immediately following that fateful evening on Mars Hill. Even now, sitting in the dim light of my basement study, examining photographs of our travels, I am having trouble piecing it together. After our time at the Pluto Dome, other than a few random snapshots of the local university and a sunset from above the clouds, there is nothing.

I have thus decided to search other photos for clues, those taken by a distinct, but not altogether different machine of exploration: the New Horizons spacecraft, first mentioned to us by the Whisperer at Lowell.

It arrived the same year as we did, in 2015, at what I will always (thanks to the creature) refer to as the Ninth *Planet.* Its flyby was anticipated and celebrated across the globe, not unlike the propitious year of Pluto's first revealing. The images sent back were stunning, the information revelatory. It was discovered, for instance, that Pluto could well have an internal ocean and that its atmosphere, like Earth's, is blue. And another prominent and distinguishing physical feature that, upon reading of it, sent my brain whirling.

I quickly pull up the photo I took of the creature in front of the informational sign, in which he appears to hold the entire planet in his palm. And there it was, a creamy marking in the lower hemisphere, in the shape of a heart. *The Heart of Pluto!*

It must have been that very shape I had found familiar, but couldn't quite articulate, when first I captured the image of them together. The New Horizon data had since revealed that the heart, officially named *Tombaugh Regio,* includes a massive, one-thousand-kilometer-wide glacier of frozen nitrogen, not unlike the kind poured on balloons in the Lowell Visitor Center. The largest such glacier known in the solar system.

As my gaze lingers on the photograph, I am riveted once again by the mysterious planet, but then my focus irresistibly drifts toward the face in orbit around it, young eyes wide and full of mischievous affection directed, like a tractor beam, toward the Old One holding the camera.

Where has he gone? I wonder.

Has he joined the rest of his kind, such as young Venitia and that Mars-loving Iowa boy who still resides in the place where books sing? I miss him terribly sometimes, though others have followed close behind, including the younger sibling of this creature who is, in many ways, just as weird. But insofar as every being, in every stage of development, is unique unto itself, there are aspects irretrievably lost in their passing, however natural.

And it is in that passing, for those of us left behind, that the answer to the question—*Are we alone?*—is finally made clear.

Or so I think.

There are footsteps on the stairs and the door opens.

"Mom says dinner is ready." It is a tall young man whose face is somehow familiar—the eyes especially—though the cheeks are now spotted with scarlet blemishes and irregular, neglected stubble. The once dirty, askew hair on the head, though still the color of straw, has been carefully combed into a great, seductive sweep above the brow. The voice, in its permanently low timbre, continues to shock.

"What are you looking at on the computer?" he asks. He approaches and leans over my shoulder, gazing at the image of the creature and the planet on the screen.

"Aw, that was a great trip. We'll have to go back sometime."

I'm afraid not, I'm tempted to say. Despite Vesto Slipher's theories of an expanding and contracting universe, there can be no actual return for us. But that is something he must discover on his own, among other creatures of his own making. He steps back toward the doorway, leading to his current life: his phone, his girlfriend, his track practice, all the less inspiring knowledge his mind must absorb in order to thrive in the future, if there is one.

But then, suddenly, he pauses and looks at me. *Those eyes!*

"Hey, Dad, remember how I used to be afraid of running hurdles? You'll be happy to know I *got over it.*"

He grins and returns up the stairs, but his words have robbed me of breath.

Can it be?

I look again at the photo, the planet resting in his palm, captured on the very doorstep of the Kuiper Zone. For that moment, and the mere dozen years preceding it, we were together, the creature and I, exploring a small portion of an amazing universe we had briefly shared. We paused, in that millisecond, to take this picture, as if directed by some supernal Intelligence beyond human understanding. Or perhaps, merely, by the young soul who, against everything I (or Slipher) had thought possible, had miraculously returned to me, just then, in yet another doorway to yet another world unknown.

As if to remind me—*Hey, Dad!*—that the secret of the ninth planet had been there all along, its truth now laid bare before my weeping eyes.

It was not the frozen heart of Pluto he forever held in his hand.

It was my own!

MY GRAPHIC MEMOIR

The Author with Pipe, in Startlement
(By His Four-Year-Old Son, Alden James Gale Price)

Ballpoint pen, on Wexford multipurpose
printer paper, 2014.

MY COURTROOM DRAMA

The Last Case

My father, Tom Price, age seventy-four, stands near the front of Webster County Courtroom Number One, in Fort Dodge, Iowa. His client, Tiffany, age forty-two, sits beside him at the table. (Some names and identifying details of people and places have been changed.)

They are waiting for the judge to enter, backs to the gallery. My father is wearing his gray tweed jacket and a white dress shirt with bow tie (the green one today). His bald, freckled head catches the overhead light and sends it back for a second. He isn't a large man, maybe five-eight; cancer surgery and late-onset diabetes have whittled down his already thin frame. Next to Tiffany, however, he looks like a giant. As he organizes his notes, she keeps her hands in the lap of her blue dress, narrow comma-bent shoulders barely extending above the edge of the table. Her straight hair is shoulder length, an artificial, inconsistent auburn. Aside from the rustling of paper, the room is silent.

This is the first hearing in what will be my father's last case, after fifty years of practicing family law. He doesn't know it yet, but it will also be one of the most difficult.

From the outside, this small-town proceeding may not appear to be on the front lines of any kind of American justice you would care enough about to defend or die for. It is a low-income divorce and custody case, involving accusations of abuse, one of thousands that largely go unnoticed every year. No celebrities or politicians. The fact that there is a trial at all is a bit of a miracle. Many women in similar circumstances will settle or appear in court without legal representation. These sorts of domestic disputes can be legally and emotionally complicated, expensive, and take a long time to resolve. For these reasons, some attorneys refuse to represent economically marginal clients like Tiffany or will demand retainers in the form of up-front cash or property liens.

Bottom line: if you commit murder in this country, you are guaranteed legal representation. If you are poor and seeking spousal support or child custody or hoping to keep the roof over your head, you're on your own.

Unless you happen to know my father.

A little background. After graduating from law school at the University of Iowa in 1963, he returned to Fort Dodge, his hometown, to begin practice. In the early 1980s, he joined the newly created Iowa Volunteer Lawyers Project, which provided pro bono services to those in need. Since then, representing low-income, disadvantaged clients has increasingly, and unexpectedly, become the center of his practice. Most have been women, many of them referred to him by the local domestic/sexual assault outreach center. He has earned a statewide reputation for being willing to take on the most desperate cases. These efforts have largely gone unpaid—a fact that has increasingly worried my sisters and me as our parents face a post-retirement reality.

But my father's choice of work (if it can be described as a choice) has little to do with money, and everything to do with the heart of the law as he understands it: to defend the defenseless. That's why he has put off retirement until his mid-seventies; he is afraid his remaining clients won't find representation.

But here it is, finally: the last client, the last unresolved promise.

When he told me this on the phone, I didn't quite believe it. When I asked about the case, he just called it a "mess." When I asked what he

meant by that, he said, well, it means that his client, Tiffany Vanderstadt, who was referred to him over a year ago, claims that her husband
physically, psychologically, and sexually abused her over the course of
decades. It means that her husband, Eddie, is a reserve police officer
who has, in turn, accused Tiffany of abusing their two children when
they were younger, and is petitioning district court for full custody
of their now adolescent son, Micah, along with child support—the
reason they are headed to trial. It means that Tiffany left Eddie and
entered the shelter, where she resided for four months. It means that
after leaving the shelter, she got a night job at a convenience store
where she was brutally assaulted during a robbery. It means she is currently working two minimum wage jobs with no financial support from
her husband, who retained all marital assets. It means she is living in
transitional public housing with their twenty-two-year-old daughter
Skylar, who supports her financially. It means she was recently charged
with eluding a pursuing police vehicle, a felony that could carry jail
time. It means that although the shelter approached other lawyers,
none would take her case.

"So why did you take it?"

"She deserves legal representation," he said. But I could tell he also
believed Tiffany was a person who had been grievously wronged.

Regardless of whether or not he is correct, this case would be the
final statement of his long career. I considered that fact for a moment, then asked if he would mind me sitting in, at least for the first
hearing. He warned me it wouldn't be very exciting. They wouldn't
be arguing child custody or spousal support. Instead, they would be
seeking an order of protection against Eddie and retention of Tiffany's
only source of transportation, a Chevy Malibu, which Eddie wants returned. Finally, they would be seeking an increase in court-determined
legal fees. Eddie has a full-time job and can afford to pay his lawyer.
Tiffany, further impoverished by divorce, has to rely on the courts to
secure the means to afford representation.

My father assured Tiffany that he would represent her no matter what the judge decides, but he told me the low-balling of the fees indicates how much the system deems her worthy of counsel—and how worthy counsel is to get paid for that effort. So far, the courts have approved $350 dollars toward her legal expenses, which covers about three hours of my father's time.

Basically, he said, this hearing would determine if Tiffany deserves fair access to justice and a life with a little more freedom and a little less fear.

I told him I'd be there.

■

Early this morning, I drove three hours from my home in western Iowa to make it to the Webster County Courthouse on time. Twenty minutes into this first hearing, however, we are still waiting for Eddie and his lawyer to make an appearance. The court reporter enters and tells my father the judge would like to see him in chambers. Tiffany, now alone at the table, turns around to see who is there. I don't recognize her, though she was apparently just a few years behind me at our high school. Her eyes lock onto Diana, a young advocate from the shelter, who nods and offers a sympathetic smile. The only other person in the courtroom is Darren, who is scheduled to testify as Tiffany's lone character witness. He's in his mid-forties, husky, wearing a navy blue suit and thick-framed glasses beneath which his eyes appear to be drowning. My father told me that Darren and his wife witnessed some of the abuse and that he has been very supportive of Tiffany.

"He may be her only friend," my father said.

Darren gives Tiffany a thumbs-up, but she lowers her eyes and turns back around.

When my father returns, he informs Tiffany that the hearing has been postponed. The opposing lawyer is on vacation and didn't bother to notify them.

■

Outside the courthouse, my father speaks briefly with Tiffany, who is wiping away tears, clearly disheartened by the delay. She leaves with Darren. With unexpected time on our hands, we decide to get a drink at a Main Street tavern near his office. This will become a tradition over the course of the trial, with all its unhappy surprises. My father has never been much of a drinker, but lately has been treating himself to the occasional whiskey in small, "diabetic" portions. At the table, he apologizes that I traveled all that way for nothing.

"This case might be another disappointment," he says. "I wouldn't blame you for not coming back."

He's referring to a trial last year, one of only two times I've seen him in court, a fact that now embarrasses me. When my sisters and I were growing up, our father didn't talk much about his work, and we didn't ask. In junior high, for career day, when I was required to write an essay on a profession that "made a positive difference in the world," I chose dentistry. So I was surprised when, during a visit home last spring, he asked if I wanted to join him for "an interesting trial." It was a common law marriage suit in which my father represented an elderly woman who had lived nearly twenty years with her farmer "husband." During her testimony, she described nursing the man she loved through the debilitating stages of Alzheimer's, which included managing the farm and, once, cleaning up after he defecated on the floor at the local café.

The Alzheimer's may have also caused him to forget her in his will, which included income and land worth well over a million dollars. Although she had no income of her own, the farmer's two adult daughters by his deceased wife were unwilling to give her anything, claiming she was just a "friend."

My father asked questions intended to establish legal recognition of a common law marriage, which in Iowa requires proving long-term cohabitation and conjugal relations, intent to be married, and public identification as husband and wife. His client tearfully recalled how she and Earl had exchanged "vows" in his pickup at sunset, and that they had planned to make things official before he became ill. And of course, *ahem*, there was only one bed in their house. He called to the stand nearly a dozen friends of the couple, some of them using walkers, to testify that theirs was indeed a very public romance, involving vacations together, hosting bridge club at their house, handholding around town, and so on. Many just assumed they were married.

It seemed a slam dunk for my father, but from where I was sitting there was even more at stake than his client's desire for hard-earned justice. With retirement nearing, and the number of paying clients dwindling, this was perhaps the last case involving a relatively large settlement. That wasn't his motivation, I knew, but I also knew that what he earned from this decision might contribute in a significant way to the degree of comfort he and my mother, after more than fifty years of life together, much of it dedicated to public service, would enjoy during the sunset years of their own marriage.

Following closing statements, the judge sent word that he was ready to deliver his verdict. He began by scolding the farmer's daughters for denying the significance of the relationship between their father and a woman he had clearly loved, a good person who had nursed their father through some very difficult times. Many testified that they behaved like a married couple in public, he continued, but unfortunately, none confirmed that either had *publicly identified* the other as husband or wife. Therefore, he was forced to deny her claim. She could retain the small house they shared in town—including a mortgage she couldn't afford—and any furniture she could prove belonged to them as a couple. Watching my father face his decimated client and then, after everyone left the courtroom, quietly pack up his briefcase, was an experience I did not care to repeat.

I don't know if this case will be another disappointment, only that it is his last. I finish my whiskey and tell him to call me when the next hearing is scheduled.

■

A month later, back in the Webster County Courthouse, I get my first look at Tiffany's husband, Eddie. He is overweight, but I can tell that underneath there is some serious muscle. His meaty neck is spilling over the collar of his dress shirt, hands resting on his belly as he leans back in his chair. Also present is his lawyer, the one who went on vacation and left us hanging. I'll call him Attorney (Atty.) Kopec. He is tall and slender and, like most lawyers in town, on friendly terms with my father, though a generation younger. They are chatting informally, and I hear him congratulate my father on his upcoming retirement, which will be official in a couple of months.

But first there is this case, the last one. Following opening statements, Atty. Kopec calls Micah to the stand. He is seventeen and has his mother's soft face and auburn hair, and his father's large build. He hunches in the witness chair, avoiding eye contact with either parent. During questioning, Micah states he is living with his father and that he would like to stay there. When asked why, he says he thinks it's a more "stable" environment. When asked why, he recounts a scene in which his mom was screaming at his dad and picked up Eddie's service revolver and put it in her mouth.

During cross-examination, my father asks Micah what he and his father do together. Micah says that his dad has taught him to shoot a gun, and they play video games. They sometimes drive around and talk. He also takes Micah to a doctor for his diabetes and to a therapist for his "anger issues." Regarding the incident with the gun, my father asks if he witnessed it. No, he heard it. He asks Micah how often he sees his mother (not very often and only in supervised visits, as ordered by the DHS) and who usually sets up those visitations (Micah does). When was their last communication? Micah says his mom sent him a text on his birthday a couple of days ago to say she loved him.

"Do you love her?" my father asks.

He says he loves both his parent, but he feels his dad can better support him.

No more questions.

Atty. Kopec calls Eddie to the stand. He states for the record that he is forty-three, and that he and Tiffany were married for almost twenty-four years before separating last October. He currently works at an appliance store but also volunteers as a reserve police officer, providing additional security for area businesses. He gets an hourly wage, but according to "tradition," he donates that money back to the department for uniforms and training. He believes everyone should give back to their community.

Eddie describes his lifestyle while married to Tiffany as "modest," by which he means they bought their clothing at Goodwill and Walmart—though he acknowledges Tiffany made a lot of the kids' clothes—and bought their food at stores using coupons, supplemented at times by Tiffany's gardening. There were no family vacations. He describes Tiffany's contributions to the family's economic well-being as minimal and implies that her recent efforts at finding a job have been half-hearted. When Tiffany left him, she took the Malibu and stuck him with the truck, which has a bad transmission. He needs reliable transportation for work and claims he can't afford to buy a new vehicle. He says he has received only $340 in child support from Tiffany.

Atty. Kopec asks Eddie to describe his current relations with his wife.

"Calm," he replies, which is how he likes it. He just wants to keep the peace; he doesn't like drama or conflict. When asked about Tiffany's behavior during their marriage, he says she broke his nose once, threw coffee in his face, hit him with a flashlight, scratched him all over. He confirms that, at one time or another, DHS was called to investigate her abuse of both children. He claims that when Skylar was in elementary school, she got in trouble for pushing another child and Tiffany spanked her bottom, leaving marks that were noticed by a caretaker. Tiffany admitted responsibility, and she was put on the child abuse registry.

Atty. Kopec asks Eddie to expound on the gun incident. He says he was on Facebook when Tiffany just attacked him, knocking him to the floor. She grabbed his service revolver and pointed it at him, then put it in her own mouth before the police intervened. In his opinion, she remains a danger to Micah.

If that's the case, Atty. Kopec continues, then why didn't you leave her earlier?

Eddie says he was raised to believe marriage is forever. And also, everyone knows the dad never gets the kids.

No more questions.

My father's cross-examination provokes only monosyllabic responses. Isn't it so, Mr. Vanderstadt, that Tiffany was in the abuse shelter for four months, during which she never received any support from you? Isn't it so that she has so far never missed a court-ordered child support payment? Isn't it the case that although you now make $56,000 a year, you have only given Tiffany a total of $700 to live on since she left the shelter? During this time, do you acknowledge that Tiffany was severely beaten during a robbery at her workplace, accumulating expensive medical bills for a broken nose, concussion, and dental work? Isn't it true, Mr. Vanderstadt, that you recently won a thousand dollars and a free trip to Las Vegas in the lottery? Isn't it true that you spent thousands on gastric bypass surgery, and yet continue your poor health habits? Isn't it also true that rather than adhering to the court order to facilitate Tiffany's access to Micah, you allow Micah to determine when to visit or talk with his mother?

"And you call Tiffany irresponsible?" There is an objection, which is sustained.

No more questions.

Atty. Kopec rests his case, and the judge recesses for lunch. My father leans over to say something to Tiffany, who sits with her head down, nodding occasionally. She leaves with daughter Skylar and friend Darren.

■

In his office, already filling up with boxes for the final move, my father surprises me by saying he felt the morning testimony went well. We're eating turkey sandwiches and apple slices sent over by "the gals from Bloomers," a café across the street. This is part of my father's daily routine: rising at five every morning, walking the same two-mile route to work, lunch at Bloomers at noon, then walking the same route home at five in the evening. My mother teases that if anyone wanted to kill him, they would know exactly where he was every hour of the workweek.

Some have threatened to do just that. As kids, there were times my sisters and I were told to play indoors because "Dad had some trouble at work." Someone once shot at him in the parking lot of the local community college, where he taught a night class in criminal law every Wednesday for more than thirty years. A couple of years ago, a fake pipe bomb was mailed to his office, which investigators suspected came from the ex-husband of a client. Just last month, someone broke into my parents' home while they were out and trashed it.

Eddie appeared to handle his cross-examination relatively well, however, coming across exactly as he described himself: calm and reasonable. I tell my father this and he shrugs it off. That's how a lot of abusers come across, he says. That's how they survive. He says testimony established that contrary to court orders, Micah, rather than Eddie or the DHS, is largely in charge of setting up visits with his mother and that the boy's primary reason for wanting to stay with his father is that he can buy him video games and guns. But then he surprises me again by saying there's little chance Tiffany will get full custody. The child abuse charges, however questionable, are still standing. Even if they were true, it is unlikely the court would acknowledge that Tiffany's diminished abilities as a parent were a consequence of Eddie's violence—such has been the case with a number of women he has represented. Tiffany is just now beginning to recover from all that.

What my father is ultimately fighting for, he says, is that Tiffany's parental rights be enforced by the court, rather than left to the whims of her ex-husband. A safe foundation on which she might begin to rebuild her relationship with her son.

I ask him why he didn't confront Eddie about the abuse. He says he's going to let Tiffany do that during her testimony.

"She's finally going to have a voice in all of this."

■

Back in court, Tiffany takes the oath, and my father asks her to please adjust the microphone that, as Eddie left it, reaches above her head. They begin.

Tiffany Vanderstadt, forty-two, states that she dropped out of high school when she was seventeen and eventually married Eddie Vanderstadt, who was a year older. "He was a nice guy at first," she says. Then he got a job at a meatpacking plant and moved Tiffany and their young daughter, Skylar, from a substandard apartment in Fort Dodge to a small rental house in the nearby rural town of Fiedler. She quickly became isolated from her friends and relatives. When Eddie quit his job at the plant to become a truck driver, he left Tiffany alone with their daughter in order to get "out-of-town training."

For more than a month, Tiffany says she had no money except for $50 her mother gave her. A relief agency in a nearby town gave her propane to heat the house, four pounds of hamburger, and enough soup to feed Skylar two meals a day. A nun from a local church gave them leftovers from the Lenten fish fry. There was government cheese.

During the next year, Eddie continued his truck driving, vanishing for weeks at a time. Tiffany got wind of on-the-road affairs. When Eddie didn't pay the rent, they were forced to leave the home in Fiedler. Tiffany's grandparents said they could rent their old farmhouse, and for the first time in a while, she was hopeful. The family would have a little land for a garden and might finally be able to put down roots. To pay expenses, Tiffany cleaned houses for about $200 a week, and she and Skylar collected cans in roadside ditches. She made it a game, telling her daughter they were helping the environment and learning about Earth Day. She felt "blessed" when they had heat, food, and clean clothes.

Tiffany got pregnant with a little boy, but he was stillborn. She wasn't sure what the causes were, perhaps a genetic defect, perhaps the well water on the acreage, which was later found to have harmful chemicals. Eddie blamed her.

When Tiffany's grandparents sold the farmhouse, the family moved to another rural town, into a former Quonset hut the "size of a garage," with part of the roof caved in. They were there for nine months. During this stretch, Eddie was fired by the trucking company, and they both picked up odd jobs: mowing lawns, raking leaves, removing fallen branches after storms. She made clothes with her grandmother's old sewing machine, including cloth diapers for their newborn son, Micah. Then Eddie moved them again, this time back to government-assisted housing in Fort Dodge. They had come full circle.

Tiffany testifies that the kids liked the new neighborhood, where they quickly made friends, which had been difficult when they were isolated in the country. She got a job and began to make a few friends of her own. That's when Eddie decided to move them all to his parents' house, in yet another rural town. Eddie's brother, along with his wife and their two kids, were also living in the house, making it a total of ten people under one roof. Eddie and Tiffany occupied a room, while their children slept in the unfinished attic. There was one bathroom, shared by all.

Eddie got a job as a corrections officer in a distant town and was gone five days a week. This went on for two years, during which Tiffany worked briefly as a waitress, but quit to care for Micah when he was diagnosed with severe asthma and diabetes. She cooked meals for the entire family, including her in-laws, cleaned the house, and did all of their laundry. The kids were unhappy. The backyard was so small "you could take scissors to it," and was often filled with garbage due to rummaging animals.

She states that whenever she complained about the conditions,

Eddie told her to "suck it up," calling her "a bitch or cunt," and that her father-in-law had once tried to punch her.

My father asks Tiffany to describe the abuse she endured during the marriage, and provides the court with photos of her swollen face taken at the hospital. She says on that particular occasion, Eddie hit her because she'd had some friends over to the house. He didn't want her to have friends. She claims he punched her, "on average," about five or six times a year. No charges were ever filed.

Tiffany says the sexual abuse started after Skylar left home and they were about to move to yet another rural house they'd purchased, this time from Eddie's best friend, Jake. To celebrate, the three of them went to a bar together and got a little drunk. During the car ride home, Eddie told Jake that, though Tiffany had lost a lot of weight, she still had nice tits and he should cop a feel. Tiffany resisted, but Eddie just laughed as his buddy stuck his hand down her shirt. Back at the house, she claims the men forced her to have sex with both of them. Eddie told her that she owed it to Jake for giving them such a sweet deal on the house. The second time they assaulted her she claims to have been drugged, and when she woke up was bleeding from her vagina and rectum. It happened two more times, she says.

The judge interrupts, "Why didn't you just go to the police?"

"I did." During the final assault, she says she managed to break free and call the police, but the officers just talked to Eddie. There were no arrests. That's when she decided to enter the shelter. She hated leaving Micah behind, but knew she wouldn't survive if she stayed. Since leaving the shelter in January, she's been living with Skylar and cleaning houses to pay child support.

"So is it safe to say," my father asks, "that nothing has changed since your husband abandoned you with no money in that house in Fiedler?"

She pauses. "Yes."

No more questions.

The judge uses this opportunity to call a recess. Eddie, grinning and shaking his head, leaves the room with his lawyer. Tiffany and my father sit down on a far bench with Diana, her advocate from the shelter. Friend Darren is hovering nearby. Tiffany's hands are shaking, and she won't look anyone in the eye. She worries aloud that she didn't do a good job telling her story. That maybe no one believes her. My father is reassuring.

"You're a courageous person," he says, and I can tell he means it.

■

When they return from recess, the judge reminds counsel they have until 4:30 p.m. to finish. My father says he has only one more witness—Darren—and since he has taken time off from work, they're hoping to squeeze him in today. Atty. Kopec agrees to delay cross-examining Tiffany until the next hearing, which I interpret as generosity.

Darren is sworn in and my father asks him to talk about his friendship with Tiffany. He says he and his wife, Tara, knew her in high school and got reacquainted at a social event. He claims to have heard about or witnessed several instances of abuse. The worst was at an auction where they saw Tiffany and Eddie arguing. He says Eddie got in his truck and side-swiped Tiffany on the way out of the parking lot. He and Tara ran over to help—Tiffany was unconscious and had to be taken to the hospital. When Darren told the police to arrest Eddie, they told him to "stay out of it." Darren and Tara spent many hours with Tiffany at the hospital. He testifies that she is a good, responsible person.

No more questions.

Atty. Kopec stands and asks Darren if he had a sexual affair with Tiffany.

My father told me earlier that he anticipated this attempt to humiliate Tiffany publicly, like so many other victims of sexual abuse who risked going to court. Tiffany had assured him that Darren was just a friend.

"Yeah, we had sex," Darren replies. "But with Eddie's blessing."

My father turns toward Tiffany, but she has put her face in her hands.

Darren is invited to elaborate. He states that after he and Tiffany had been friends for a while, he told her he wanted more. Although Darren and his wife had an open relationship at the time, he believed getting Eddie's consent was the honorable thing to do. He sent Tiffany to ask him about it, and they got the green light. On the night of their "date," Eddie left a bottle of wine in Tiffany's car, along with a box of condoms and a note that said, "Have fun!" Afterward, Eddie asked Darren for details, but he refused to share any. That would have been disrespectful to Tiffany.

The back of my father's head has turned the color of a blood moon.

Darren adds that Tiffany is just a friend now, and that he and his wife are no longer swingers. They're "together."

No more questions.

After adjourning, the judge calls both lawyers into chambers. When my father returns, I watch from a distance as he confronts Tiffany and her "character witness" just outside the courtroom.

"*You,*" he says, pointing at Darren. "I don't ever want to see you again."

Darren starts to protest, but my father interrupts: "*Get the hell out of here!*"

As Darren leaves, my father faces Tiffany.

"You *lied* to me!"

"I'm so sorry," she says, leaning on Diana's shoulder, sobbing. Skylar is also there, holding her hand.

"That's not good enough!" my father replies, his raised voice echoing across the arched, glass-paneled ceiling of the century-old courthouse.

"I'm trying to get your life back and you *lie* to me? Is there anything else you've lied about, because if there is, you'd better tell me now or I'm *done.*"

"No," she says, still not looking at him. "I'm so sorry."

"*Jesus*. You finally had the chance to tell your side of the story, and now that's destroyed. Eddie and his lawyer couldn't be happier, I can tell you that."

I think my father is finished, and I'm relieved because he's seventy-four, and I worry about his heart. He walks toward the stairs, pauses, then returns to Tiffany.

"Go home," he says, calmer now. "Think about what happened here today. Talk to Diana—she'll be nicer about it than I was—and get it straight in your mind what you want out of all of this. This is about *your* future. Think about that, and we'll talk. We have one more hearing. We'll work it out. It'll be OK."

She nods into Diana's shoulder.

"I'm so sorry."

"I know you are," he says.

■

I can tell my father doesn't feel much like chatting at the tavern. He says he regrets raising his voice with Tiffany—she's been yelled at enough in her life—but there was all that work, and they were so close to getting something good for her out of this mess.

"It's time for me to retire," he says. "This proves it. What a way to end."

It's a bad moment for him, and I want to say something helpful. I recall how, just following Tiffany's testimony, I thought she was right to worry whether or not anyone believed her—the judge certainly seemed skeptical. Even if the judge appreciated the difficulties women face when trying to leave abusers, the sheer amount of abuse and degradation she described, over the course of nearly twenty-five years, might prove too difficult for him, or any outsider, to fully accept. But then Darren took the stand, someone supposedly on Tiffany's side, her "only friend," and confirmed just how degraded she had been.

I share this with my father. He thanks me for my perspective but isn't sure they can get anything for her at this point. We finish our drinks and walk home. My mother greets us cheerily at the door and asks how the hearing went.

"I'll let John tell you about it," he says, and walks upstairs to lie down for a few minutes before supper, which is meatloaf.

■

It is a strange thing to witness a man confront the limits of his own lifetime of labor, for which there has been so much sacrifice, so much striving and stress, so much investment of self. And then to see it all become embodied for that man in a last effort that he believes will be a failure. And then for that man to be your father.

It was a little too much for me, and I confess that during the intervening weeks I was tempted to come up with an excuse not to attend the final hearing. But then I find myself, once again, on the third floor of the Webster County Courthouse.

While my father visits the restroom, I consider the fact that his career is about to end in the exact spot where it began. He told me earlier that today's hearing will take place in the same courtroom where he went, over fifty years ago, to consider whether or not he wanted to be a lawyer. He was nearing graduation from Iowa State Teachers College (now the University of Northern Iowa), and had planned to teach high school history. During one of his college classes, he became fascinated with the impact lawyers and judges have had on American social justice. He devoured *To Kill a Mockingbird*, as well as the biographies and writings of Learned Hand, Thurgood Marshall, and fellow Iowan Joseph Welch, the attorney who took down Joseph McCarthy with the famous words, "At long last, have you left no sense of decency?"

Whatever their fears and flaws, these historic lawmen, like those in the movie westerns my father loved as a boy—still loved—had fulfilled their responsibility to show up and face the bad guys.

At the time, my mother, then a nursing student and his fiancée, encouraged him to look into the possibility of law school. He told her he wasn't confident he had the ability. The grandson of a Missouri coal miner, he spent his childhood in rural Kansas and didn't learn to read until the third grade, due in part to undiagnosed dyslexia. When he told his parents he was considering law school, his mother strongly discouraged him from taking the risk. That summer in 1959, he walked up these stairs and into courtroom number one, with its high ceilings and balustrades and ornate woodwork, to reflect on whether or not he could see himself there. Whether or not he could make a difference, like the legal heroes he had read about and admired. He was twenty years old.

Now he's seventy-four and about to enter that same courtroom for the last time, asking, in a way, the same questions.

I wonder if that's why he's taking so long in the bathroom, though it's more likely his prostate. It's been giving him trouble again, and he'll soon have corrective surgery. It was a prostate exam a few years ago that revealed the tumor on his kidney, which the surgeon said would have killed him within the year. I look at the wall of photos of deceased members of the local Iowa Bar Association. Many of the faces are familiar—they populate the story of my time living here, and my father's. There's his high school best friend and first law partner who suffered early dementia and died in his fifties; there's his final law partner, a long-time neighbor whose children I grew up with. Last year, he fell down the basement stairs, hit his head, and died. My father discovered the body, worried after he didn't show up for work. I see more pictures of his friends and colleagues and realize that my father may be the last of his generation still practicing law in this town.

The last one standing. And it's high noon.

We take our places in the courtroom, and Atty. Kopec calls Tiffany to the stand for cross-examination, which was delayed to allow my father the favor of Darren's testimony. His initial questions focus on Tiffany's sexual immorality and how she and Darren betrayed the trust of her husband. He then recites the litany of abuse allegations against her, and restates the fact that the DHS, supported by Juvenile Court, has ordered that her visits with Micah be supervised. He mentions her arrest for eluding a police vehicle.

A lot of time is then spent on the fact that Tiffany hasn't contributed in any major way to the financial support of her family. She replies that she has applied for several higher paying jobs but was turned down because she is on the child abuse registry. She adds that she has recently gotten a second job as a front desk receptionist at a hotel for twenty-five hours a week at $7.25 an hour. She has been told she can pick up extra hours busing tables at the hotel restaurant. Atty. Kopec asks about her living arrangements, and she confirms that she still resides with her daughter, who is helping support her. Is she presently involved in a relationship? No.

"Given all this, you are still seeking primary physical care of Micah?"

"Yes."

No more questions.

My father stands and gets right to Tiffany's history with Darren. It began two years ago, she says, when she and Eddie were at a karaoke bar. While there, she ran into Darren and his wife, Tara, whom she had known since middle school. They were friendly to her, and she was desperate for friends. The couples began to hang out together. On New Year's Eve, Darren and Tara invited her and Eddie to go swimming at a hotel. Later, in one of the rooms, she claims Eddie and Tara had loud sex in the shower while she and Darren watched TV. Tiffany states that she felt "backed into a corner" from the pressure they all continued to put on her to participate in their swinging. She eventually relented.

When my father asks if sex with Darren was about pleasure, she begins to sob.

"No," she replies. "I was so ashamed and told him to stop!"

She says she never had sex with Darren again, but he continued to involve himself in her life. What she doesn't say, but told my father earlier, is that she'd lied to him about Darren because she feared losing her son forever—a threat Eddie had always used to control her. She worried Darren's character testimony might be her only hope. My father told her she still should have trusted him, but apparently, trust is just another thing she's been robbed of.

On the stand, he asks Tiffany why she didn't leave Eddie at this point, why she didn't permanently break from Darren, why she didn't try to escape the whole awful situation.

"I had no place to go, no money, no friends. I felt like dirt. I beat myself up every day."

The subject shifts to the child abuse allegations. She says she loves her children and never abused them, but claims Eddie did, numerous times. She says he pressured her to take the blame in order to protect his job and benefits, which they needed to afford Micah's medical treatments.

Regarding her arrest for eluding a police vehicle, Tiffany says the incident occurred a month after she entered the abuse shelter. Although Eddie had been ordered by the court not to have physical contact with her, she claims he'd repeatedly followed her in his squad car. She says he once blocked her from leaving a parking lot, shouting "Do us all a fucking favor and just put a bullet in your head!"—something she had almost done during the infamous revolver incident. On this occasion, Tiffany was leaving Walmart and noticed a police cruiser parked nearby, with a driver that looked like Eddie. When she sped out of the parking lot, the cruiser followed. Tiffany panicked and stepped on the accelerator. The cruiser gave chase, sirens blaring. While racing through the streets of town, she dialed 911 on her cell phone, screaming that her husband was finally going to kill her. The dispatcher eventually convinced her to pull off the road, where the officer drew his gun and cuffed her. She was terrified.

My father got her out of jail, but when he later asked the police department for the 911 recording, he was told it had been accidentally erased. The charges were soon reduced, but (as my father put it) the message had been sent: *you will never escape.*

Before she steps down from the stand, he has one last question: "Tiffany, what do you want out of all of this?"

She starts crying again.

"I want to move on ... build a life. I used to have plans."

The rest of the afternoon testimony moves quickly. Skylar takes the stand and backs up her mother's version of events. She insists that it was her father who hit her when she was a child and that he had frightened her into lying to the police and social workers. Did she ever see her mother strike her father or Micah? No. After she left home, Skylar says she tried to get the abuse charges against her mother revoked, but was told too many years had elapsed. She currently works at a convenience store, is engaged to be married, and wants to be a minister. She pays most of the expenses related to living with Tiffany, and says she is happy to do so until her mom can get back on her feet. Just like she took care of them all those years.

Atty. Kopec calls Eddie to the stand to deny everything, which he does. My father follows with a final summary of Eddie's crimes against Tiffany and their children, then rests his case.

The judge concludes the hearing by addressing Tiffany and Eddie. He says that he has never encountered a case with such divergent versions of the truth and regrets that their behavior has led to so much collateral damage involving their children. He acknowledges that they both had good lawyers, however, and applauds counsel for not making a bad situation worse. On a personal note, he says he feels this case has brought him full circle as a judge. During his first case on the bench some twenty-five years ago, Tom Price represented one of the litigants.

"Now unless Tom is Brett Favre, this will be the last time he and I will lock horns. I want him to know that it has been an honor and a privilege, and to thank him for his service."

Then it's over.

■

Months later, after my father has officially retired, there is a ruling, a copy of which he mails to me.

Although allegations of spousal abuse are deemed "he said/she said," the findings of child abuse against Tiffany, and Micah's own preference, cannot be ignored. Custody is given to Eddie, but with the order that regular visitations occur and that the Department of Human Services "undertake all efforts to restore a trusting relationship" between Micah and his mother. Regarding child support, the judge acknowledges that Tiffany's current "earning capacity is somewhat restricted," and sets her contribution at $250 per month, which is less than what Eddie wanted, and will continue until Micah graduates from high school. Eddie will be required to pay Micah's health insurance and the majority of any excess health costs.

The judge also finds that, given the disparity in income, short-term "rehabilitative alimony" is justified. Eddie is required to pay Tiffany $500 a month until Micah graduates, minus Tiffany's child-support obligations of $250, and $400 a month for two additional years. This adds up to $15,600 over four years. In addition, Tiffany gets to keep the Chevy Malibu and half of Eddie's IPERS employment retirement benefits. Eddie is required to pay $1,000 toward Tiffany's legal costs and is warned that any further violation of the no-contact order will result in incarceration.

"Does this mean you won?" I ask my father on the phone.

"Well, Tiffany is happy," he says. "She's free to start rebuilding her relationship with Micah. The alimony isn't much, but it gives her a chance."

I'm skeptical but can hear the relief in his voice. Like his client, he's about to start the next chapter of his life. He has plans again. Visiting the grandkids with my mother, taking long walks with the dog, attending church, watching back-to-back TV westerns, reading the many books that have piled up over the years. Meatloaf. This is the way many in our family will remember him.

But I will also remember him that other way, in the moments just after the final hearing, when he and Tiffany stood behind the rail that separated them—and all that their brief relationship implies about the long human struggle for justice—from the rest of us.

As he packed up his briefcase for the last time, everyone was standing. They were leaving the courtroom, moving on to other things, but that's not how I saw it.

What I saw were people standing because, well, my father was passing by.

MY ARCHAEOLOGICAL DIG SITE

Among the Ruins of Bethsaida
(On Thirty Years of Teaching Creative Nonfiction)

Yesterday, like almost every day after teaching, I walked by the ruins of Bethsaida. Or rather, a few artifacts in a small, glassed-in hallway display and adjacent exhibit room.

For many years, the University of Nebraska at Omaha, where I direct the English Department's Creative Nonfiction Writing Program, oversaw the archaeological recovery of that ancient city in what is now the Golan Heights of Israel. Dominating the exhibit is the stele (or arched stone marker) depicting the Moon God, a bull-faced deity with horns the shape of a crescent moon. The stele was originally located at the inner gateway to the walled city and dates back to when Bethsaida, founded in the tenth century BCE, served as the capital of the kingdom of Geshur.

This Moon God, as the informational sign explains, was among the most important in Mesopotamia and reigned over darkness and simultaneously "created light, the sun, and the world."

Bethsaida was destroyed in 732 BCE by the king of Assyria and subsequently fell under the jurisdiction of many different rulers and civilizations, many different gods. Jesus is said to have performed mighty works there, including healing a blind man and walking on water and feeding five thousand with only five loaves and two fish. It was the home of at least three of his disciples, and the place where he called on them to become fishers of men.

A few centuries later, floods and tectonic activity caused the Sea of Galilee to retreat south. The once vibrant city dried up, and in another few centuries, its location became so completely forgotten it was believed by some to be a figment of story and imagination. Until it was rediscovered beneath the sand and rock in 1987 by a University of Nebraska scholar, Rami Arav. For years, Professor Arav enlisted UNO faculty and students to help at the dig site, and the exhibit includes a few of their journals and scrap books.

I was not among those faculty who visited Bethsaida, but yesterday I carried with me, as if in one of the cracked offering vessels at the foot of the Moon God, a sentence from a student essay I'd just read that made me reconsider the distance. It was written by a woman who had been physically abused by her husband, and the line was: "After months of wandering in the rubble, I knew I needed to rebuild."

You'd think after thirty years of teaching what is now broadly called "creative nonfiction," I'd be more prepared for a line like that, which, divorced from the essay or from the life, is pretty ordinary. But such a divorce is no longer possible for me, if it ever was. That is partly a consequence of the history of my own education as a writer and teacher, which I hold dear, and which I sometimes fear will, like Bethsaida, be lost if I do not in some way commemorate it.

As many others have observed, creative nonfiction is a relatively new term applied to a very old form, which might loosely be defined as fact-based nonfiction that uses creative writing techniques. The label has been retroactively applied to such diverse historical forms as personal essays, memoirs, travel writing, nature writing, narrative nonfiction, lyric essays, speculative nonfiction, prehistoric cave drawings (the first graphic memoirs?), and multiple other subgenres my students encounter every day, in print or online, but don't think twice about.

Literary taxonomies certainly have their usefulness, but I tell my students that they should also think of literary forms, as with living creatures, in terms of how they behave and interact and reproduce—for art of all sorts does indeed reproduce and evolve over generations and centuries.

What do these forms have to teach us about certain ways of being in the world?

When it comes to creative nonfiction—or "literary nonfiction," as some prefer to call it—my answer has a lot to do with the habitat in which I first encountered it. I count myself among the initial generations of university students, in the 1980s and 90s, to be trained specifically to write and teach creative nonfiction. Not as a sideshow to our primary careers as novelists or poets or scholars or journalists or celebrities, but as our primary calling and craft, for which we earned advanced degrees in creative nonfiction (a term that first achieved popularity during that time), and who then occupied newly created teaching positions in creative nonfiction.

At the University of Iowa, when I first arrived as a freshman in 1984, the famous Writers' Workshop did not offer nonfiction courses—not unusual in creative writing programs at the time. That was left to a group of visionary faculty in the English Department, led by Carl H. Klaus, most of whom were scholars in literature and rhetoric. They shared, however, a passion for artfully crafted nonfiction and a growing desire to elevate it from an introductory exercise in composition classrooms, where it had been stranded since the 1960s, to its rightful place among the great literary forms. And to offer students a chance to study, practice, and teach that art.

I was one of those students. As an undergraduate from a smallish Iowa town, I arrived on campus intending to study the sciences and go on to medical school, which made my grandmother very happy. I was also a big fan of the television medical drama *St. Elsewhere*, and wanted to be just like Denzel Washington—still do. And I wanted to heal people and be rich. While fulfilling those pesky general education humanities classes, however, I encountered, without knowing it, several creative nonfiction writers who also happened to be scientists: Primo Levi (chemist), Rachel Carson (marine biologist), and Loren Eiseley (anthropologist).

Somehow, reading these people didn't feel like a required assignment. It felt more essential, like breathing.

The first opportunity I had to write creative nonfiction myself, outside of that introductory composition assignment, was in an advanced writing course taught by Professor Paul Diehl in the summer of 1987—less than a year away from graduation and (I assumed) medical school, where I planned to become a pediatrician. The previous semester, Professor Diehl's literature class on lyric structures in poetry had transformed my relationship to language, which, as an extreme though functioning introvert, had mostly been a source of fear and embarrassment. Professor Diehl apparently detected the small needle of potential in this student's unexceptional haystack, and invited me to join his summer class, which was a slight violation of the rules, since it was a graduate course.

Here was an important, early example of the kind of teacher who is willing to risk dishonoring academic "rigor," that they might better honor the talents of their students.

That said, the graduate students in this class were all brilliant, dedicated nonfiction writers, and I sensed the first day that I was way out of my depth. During the next several weeks, I did my best to compose an essay about my ongoing job as a nursing assistant for children with developmental disabilities, some of them terminally ill. I had originally taken this job to boost my resume for medical school, but over the years, my experiences with these children had transformed me in profound ways I only first articulated on those pages. The essay was read and discussed—my first experience with serious workshopping—and the responses, in addition to improving the prose, invited me to more closely examine the personal reasons behind that work.

This is another of the many possible definitions of creative nonfiction: using memory and language to trace our ethical lives back to their sources. To cross the distance between the *then* and the *now*, uncovering meaning to share.

That process, with that particular essay, led me to revisit the still-birth of my brother in 1974 and the feelings I had been carrying inside me, largely unacknowledged, since I was seven years old. With each child I worked with in that hospital, and all those imagined future pediatric patients, I wondered if, in part, I was making up for some personal failing I thought had led to my brother's death. I hadn't been good enough, and never would be.

Maybe it was time to let that go.

While I don't consider creative nonfiction writing to be therapy—there are other degrees for that—its cathartic, personally transformative dimensions should never be dismissed. I'm a living example. In the end, that class taught me a lot about the more technical aspects of good writing, which are valuable in any profession, as English Departments frequently trumpet on their websites. But what it also taught me was less easily measured: that the practice of medicine is not the only healing art. A fragment of the human story, previously hidden, revealed and shaped through artful writing by the one who actually lived it, for those who had not, might also claim that ability. For both reader *and* writer.

Soon after, to my grandmother's bitter disappointment, I dropped pre-med and applied to the graduate program in English at Iowa. At the time, their degree in nonfiction writing was called the Master of Arts with an Emphasis in Expository Writing, or "MAW." Not an ideal acronym, but I have since learned to appreciate how creative nonfiction programs in their infancy often have to learn to live and grow, like hermit crabs, inside the calcified shells of more traditional academic structures. Until they are free to create structures of their own.

And that's exactly what happened. Over the next decade, the program would transform into one of the first stand-alone MFA programs in nonfiction writing in the country, and I would be among its first graduates. We students learned much by watching our mentors, in the guise of both shepherds and warriors, strive to elevate the program to equal status among advanced degrees offered by our university, advocating for precious (and often jealously guarded) resources and faculty lines. It was a cause aided by the excellent teaching in the program, which resulted in excellent student writing and, later, excellent books.

Harder to measure, however, are the ways their teaching improved the quality of our lives, calling us to set forth and become our own kinds of fishers.

Which brings me to another professor of mine at Iowa, Richard Lloyd-Jones. A Victorianist by training, his primary professional interests were in rhetoric, composition, and the teaching of writing, for which he had earned national recognition and awards. I knew none of that when I signed up for his class in the fall of 1990, titled "Rhetorical Theory, Analysis, and Application." I was twenty-four and, unfortunately, this would be the only course I would take with him, since he was nearing retirement.

On the first day of class, he invited us to call him "Jix" (a surprising intimacy during that era), and all I can say of my initial impression is that he instantly put me at ease. Perhaps it was the bearded, grandfatherly appearance or the pixie-ish smile that rarely wavered, even as he seemed to struggle to breathe. I would later find out he was operating with only part of a lung, due to a teenage bout with bronchiectasis. Every sentence seemed to cost him—but what sentences! They were brilliant and eloquent, yes, but I would also soon learn to appreciate their informing kindness and curiosity and good humor.

There was laughter in that theory classroom, which is no small accomplishment.

The text we used was *The Rhetorical Tradition: Readings from Classical Times to the Present*, a huge tome with thin, semi-transparent pages that made reading them feel like riding a canoe on the surface of an ocean, constantly aware of the depths beneath the oars. Those were some tough waters for me—Aristotle, Locke, Cereta, Nietzsche,

Bakhtin, Foucault, Cixous—but it helped to have such a knowledgeable and patient guide. I knew that during the next class, Jix would inevitably bring these luminaries back to earth with his go-to question: "So why does any of this matter?" During our often-digressive discussions, that was always the orienting issue for him: the application, the relevancy. And most of all, the ways we might use these ideas to become more intentional and helpful as writers, teachers, and moral actors in the world. Everything else was secondary to that quest.

This included, it seemed, his grading policy, which was never mentioned (that I can recall) and would have felt almost blasphemous in a class dedicated to the majesty and ethical power of language. I wrote my final paper on the rhetorician Kenneth Burke and received my first and only A+ in a graduate course. I can't recall why I was initially drawn to Burke, perhaps because the introduction in our book claimed he was "vigorously attacked by both literary critics and rhetoricians for muddling literature and nonliterature, poetic and rhetoric, language and life."

Much like our professor did every day in class.

I didn't appreciate it then, but that course was good preparation for the challenges facing me and other creative nonfiction writers and teachers in the years ahead, many of whom would be vigorously attacked for their own muddling of language and life. In the mid 1990s, even as the *New York Times Sunday Magazine* declared it "The Age of the Literary Memoir" and my fellow students were signing lucrative book contracts, there was sometimes an awe-inspiring backlash in newspapers and magazines against "the fourth genre." This includes a still infamous piece in *Vanity Fair* by Michael Shnayerson, titled "Women Behaving Badly," which implied that popular memoirs by several featured women, some of whom focused on abuse, might be the result of unresolved psychological problems and/or a petty desire to take advantage of a hot memoir market.

Public criticism was also directed at teachers and institutions that offered courses in creative nonfiction, still relatively rare at the time.

In 1997, on his show *Politically Incorrect*, Bill Maher and his guests skewered college professors teaching memoir writing to students who, they claimed, had experienced little worth writing about. "An exercise in licking the mirror," they deemed it.

Even one of the candidates for the English Department's first official creative nonfiction hire said, during his visit with students, that he preferred to get personal writing "out of the way" early in the semester then move to more "serious," research-intensive forms such as the cultural criticism he wrote—because, you know, it's all nonfiction. He said this without hesitation or apology to a group of people, ranging from their twenties to their fifties, who were seeking guidance on how to write effectively about personal experiences with, among other things, clinical depression and physical disability and the death of a parent. In contrast, his most recent area of serious research was Barbara Walters.

It is sometimes hard to explain to students in one of the many creative nonfiction courses currently offered in my department, and elsewhere, what it was like back then to be studying, writing, and teaching this form while pursuing our degrees. Equally difficult to explain are the challenges that awaited some of us on the other side of graduation. Getting an academic job was no small thing, and still isn't. But then came the sometimes lonely task of building programs from virtually nothing, with little or no resources; founding and editing journals that published nonfiction; organizing and funding (sometimes out of our own pockets) visiting author series; creating entire catalogs of new curriculum; advocating for the genre (and for its writers seeking promotion) among colleagues and administrators who had little knowledge of the field; and working locally/regionally/nationally/internationally to demonstrate the importance of personal stories as a way into social, cultural, and ecological knowledge and understanding. A way into witness.

Today, what seems normal to many in English and creative writing programs is to some of us from that earlier time a miracle—not unlike the loaves and fishes—but one that was the result of Herculean efforts by people we knew and cared about. Still care about.

Most importantly, amid all that, we were trying to mentor our own students as they sought to craft meaningful, public art out of some of the most intensely private experiences. Over the years, I tried one organized pedagogy or another, but ultimately kept returning to what Jix and some of my other nonfiction teachers taught me: to humble yourself to the text and to its author. To fully immerse in the vision laid out before you on the page and to find, within that vision, while acknowledging your own potential biases, the standards and expectations it has created for itself. Then to do your best—through critical analysis, but also informed compassion and improvisation—to help that piece live up to its potential, as you interpret it, to transform both writer *and* reader.

For that to occur, I was taught, the work should hold a deep urgency for the teacher, as it does for the writer—even if the writer cannot yet fully articulate that urgency, as I couldn't in that first essay about being a nursing assistant. The work, and the individual life that informs it, should be invited to enter the core of our being and take hold because, we must tell ourselves, this civilization, this world depends on it. Or at least the person seated at that desk in the third row does.

To be trusted with these personal stories and experiences, year after year, is a tremendous privilege, but on some days it feels like something else altogether.

Far from being a "voyeur" (as another 1990s *Vanity Fair* article called memoir readers), I sometimes think I resemble the shape-shifting alien in Ray Bradbury's *The Martian Chronicles*, himself from a lost civilization, who is transformed into the person most loved or hated by the humans around him, until he vanishes entirely under the weight of their desires. High up among those desires, I have found—and I felt it as a student also—is that the creative nonfiction teacher become the long-awaited, ideal reader, the one who might not just offer technical advice, but also become the gateway to validation and perhaps publication. The one who will help ensure that their stories—and the life from which they are born—will not be ignored or dismissed or lost or forgotten.

How can I explain to those students or to anyone that their stories, published or not, are never lost? I carry them with me, always.

Just this week, there came back to me three of those stories, those lives—each written on the cusp of distinctly new eras in the history of a civilization. The first occurred when I was purchasing a pastry at our student center, and it had some powdered sugar on it. I was suddenly reminded of the student in the fall of 2001 who wrote a personal essay about 9/11 and being middle-aged and sacrificing most of her personal life in order to take care of her aging mother. The week following the attacks, with all the reports of powdered anthrax, she opened two boxes of chicken potpies—the only dinner she could afford some nights, due to her mother's medical bills and other expenses—to find it full of a white powdery substance. She slumped sobbing to the floor, panicked that she would die in that kitchen, cooking potpies for her mother instead of having a life, and called the first response terrorism unit. They soon showed up in their hazmat suits and removed the suspicious substance, which of course turned out to be flour.

Not very long after reading that piece, I watched a local news report on some of the more "unusual" calls to the terrorism unit, which included the potpie incident, but not the story of the aging mother or the medical bills or the vanished personal life.

The second occurred when I entered the men's bathroom on the third floor. I once again avoided the far stall, because a student of mine from a wealthy family in west Omaha had once written about how, after back surgery, he had become addicted to prescribed painkillers and then heroin—well before the national opiate scourge was described as such by mainstream media. This student wrote about how, in that very stall, he had injected heroin into one of his only remaining, viable veins, which was in his penis. For him, it was the moment of complete ruination, when he realized he had "roamed in the rubble too long and needed to rebuild," which he did.

Now I look on that stall much the same as I look on the remains of Bethsaida, with the sense that something at once horrifying and sacred took place there. I won't step inside it.

The third occurred while teaching a class, simply noticing a desk in the third row that had once been occupied by a quiet, middle-aged, middle school substitute teacher who wrote about nothing more dramatic than his love of teaching, community theatre, and family. A year or so later he took his own life. And yet I can still see him sitting there, hear the words of the essay he read on the final day of class—a work of art, a voice, never to be heard again on this earth.

Is this any less important than the fall of empires?

When I think of personal writing teachers who began their careers around the same time I did (or even earlier), I wonder if their days are spent, like mine, roaming through the fragments of such stories, and the memories and wisdom and emotions they evoke. I wonder if we have become a kind of living archaeological site where, inside us, hidden even from ourselves, are the accumulated stories of all the students we've worked with, all the lives we've entered, however briefly, to witness both misery and miracle. Together, we have mentored thousands of these students as they toiled over their sentences, their scenes, their articulated thoughts and feelings and experiences. I wonder if it is true that the life stories we read become in some way a part of our own, completing the grand exercise of compassion that we are told literature is capable of and which, as some of us believe, is its primary purpose.

If so, then over these last thirty years my life has been expanded thousand-fold, tearing down walls and broadening the boundaries of what I might, in some other vocation, have naively considered an individual self.

Within those expanded boundaries, I have vicariously experienced numerous awkward, funny, inspiring, sometimes disturbing family gatherings. I have attended countless funerals and weddings and births and doctor appointments. I have met and loved and grieved every kind of pet imaginable. I have journeyed to beautiful and frightening places, across oceans and in backyards, in old cars and new, in combines and semi-trucks, on bicycles and motorcycles and airplanes, some of which were dropping bombs. I have made love in too many places, in too many ways, with too many people, to possibly recall. I have been married and divorced and remarried and divorced again. I have been lesbian, gay, bi, trans, and ace, and been loved as such, but also, as such, been beaten and ostracized and cursed and condemned to hell. I have remained celibate until the night of my sixtieth birthday. I have been a monk who studied wild turkeys, found faith, and lost it, and found it again. I've had visions of Jesus and Mary and Buddha, recited the Quran, seen the ghosts of ancestors standing at the foot of my bed, and worshipped trees and rocks. I've lost a teenage son in a car crash, adopted sons and daughters, been adopted myself and found my biological parents. I've given birth and had abortions, and been someone who wished they'd never been born. I've been paralyzed and suffered malaria, Lyme disease, breast cancer, cervical cancer—every kind of cancer—a variety of STDs, the full spectrum of mental illness, Crohns and celiac disease and diabetes-induced blindness, and achieved a full body of tattoos. I've lost my job, worked three jobs, night and day jobs, labor and desk jobs, and still been hungry and full of dreams. I have felt the rage and betrayal and violence of racism. I've been sexually abused by strangers and family members and priests and coaches and employers and neighbors and friends. I have been incarcerated and been set free.

I have died and not gone into the light.

So it continues. With every personal story I read—such as this latest abuse story—there is this opening and excavation, the new words, the new life uncovering other experiences I've read about or remembered, other ways of telling and the new ways they make me see and know and feel. Every time, I ask: How can I help this newly encountered temple of prose draw strength from what has come before, and yet distinguish itself, build itself to the sky, temporary though we know it all to be? How can I assist this word architect in creating something that will last and be remembered by more than a few people in a classroom? How might that work of art unlock hidden rooms inside readers, that the vision can make a home there and do its necessary work? How can I—despite my own limitations—make a home for that vision inside me, where I can preserve and honor it? Honor them.

To do so means, within myself, to become transformed—to build and be destroyed and rebuild—with each essay or memoir I encounter. Each student.

■

Now, if I were back in that graduate rhetorical theory class, this might be the point when Jix gently interrupts and draws me back to the text at hand, perhaps by Kenneth Burke (whose ideas have stuck with me, despite the decades and fuzzy grading policy), reintroducing the question: "Why does any of this matter?"

Being no expert in Burke, but encouraged by our professor to "make him our own," I might draw liberally from the selected readings for that day, beginning with the selection from A *Rhetoric of Motives* (1950), where he asks, "What is involved when we say what people are doing and why they are doing it?"

Burke's answer involves clarifying the "resources of ambiguity" that lead to "transformation" and "alchemical opportunity," all while acknowledging that, unlike in some "theological notions of creations and recreations"—including perhaps the miracles of a Moon God or a Christ—"in reality, we are capable of but partial acts, acts that but partially represent us and that produce but partial transformations."

Nevertheless, such partial representations and symbolic acts—including, he argues, literature and "personal statements about the loveable and the hateful"—cannot be dismissed as "nonsense." When skillfully rendered, they can lead not just to "persuasion" in a reader, but "identification." They are, in themselves, "real words, involving real tactics, having real demonstrable relationships. And as such, a study of their opportunities, necessities, and embarrassments would be central to the study of human motives."

I might then move on to the assigned selection from *Language as Symbolic Action* (1966), specifically Burke's theory of the "terministic screen"—a selected or received "nomenclature" that "necessarily directs the *at*tention into some channels rather than others" and therefore shapes, even determines, our individual and collective "reality."

Clearly the ruins of Bethsaida—or more accurately, the way they have been organized into a grammar within this exhibit, within the "symbolic environment" of a hallway located physically and culturally within a metropolitan midwestern university and received and interpreted by a white, cis-gendered, middle-aged, middle-class professor—have become a terministic screen through which I have come to view the "reality" of my actions as a teacher of creative nonfiction writing. This terministic screen has helped me articulate, but also seemingly contain, an individually experienced reality that, like all those who have come before, in countless civilizations, alive and dead, is ultimately partial, inarticulate, and uncontainable.

It has likewise done so by directing "*at*tention" away from certain channels and their competing notions of "reality." This includes deflection from what Burke identifies as "the very scientific ideals of an 'impersonal' terminology" that, as in the case of the Hitlerite Empire, "can contribute ironically to such disaster: for it is but a step from treating inanimate nature as mere 'things' to treating animals, and then enemy peoples, as mere things. But they are not mere things, they are persons—and in the systematic denial of what one knows in his heart to be the truth, there is a perverse principle that can generate much anguish."

"Indeed," he continues, "the very 'global' conditions that call for greater identification of all men with one another have at the same time increased the range of human conflict, the incentives to division. It would require sustained rhetorical effort, backed by the imagery of a richly humane and spontaneous poetry, to make us fully sympathetic with people in circumstances greatly different from our own."

Is this why the writing and teaching of creative nonfiction matters?

Is it—or can it be—a richly humane, spontaneously poetic antidote to the worst within and between those of us who belong to what Burke calls "the often-inhuman human species"?

"*Why not?*" Jix might say, with that pixie-ish smile.

■

Across the distance between that class and this hallway, between that unfortunately deceased teacher and his temporarily living student— between the *then* and the *now*—I might introduce yet another, final terministic screen, a more recent discovery at the Bethsaida dig site, which is not mentioned in the hallway exhibit.

I read about it last year in *UNO Magazine,* a short article under the title "Finding Romeo and Juliet." It included a photo of two entwined skeletons, an archaeological uncovering that was "the first of its kind in the region, and possibly only the third of its kind in the world—two teenagers, buried together in an apparent embrace." Although Professor Arav, the director of excavations, clarifies that they have "no clue who this couple is or why they were buried together"—did they have experiences "worth" writing about?—their skeletal remains were named after the famous romantic couple because they were discovered during the week of Valentine's Day.

As Burke might say, regardless of original motivations, there is now established a "real" relationship between the symbol and the recipient of the symbol, between the bones and the people at the dig site, and now me. A relationship with new (but equally mysterious) motivations that are now open to new (but equally partial) interpretations, one of which might be that those bones have been granted a sympathetic story of intimacy and identification because, in the end, that is what we hope for ourselves and for those whom we love.

To that I would add my own, more selfish hope: that to every discovery of artful, personal witness, the written words of which might be seen as yet another mysterious collection of bones, readers will grant a story of caring between a teacher and a student.

Regardless, Bethsaida may soon face yet another extinction. Professor Arav has retired from UNO, and our faculty and students no longer work at the dig site. By wintertime, I was recently told, the exhibit I have passed for the last five years will be moved to a college out east and some of the artifacts returned to the Ministry of Antiquities in Israel. The physical memory of this ancient city, its fragments and bones, its stories, will be lost to future generations of students and faculty walking these halls. Bethsaida will no longer be called, daily, into their consciousness or conveniently offered up as a terministic screen through which to view and partially understand human experience. Its sacred stele and offering bowls will be placed within another temporary civilization, another walled fortress of learning and sacrifice, another hallway—another symbolic environment—full of its own opportunities, necessities, and embarrassments. Its own stories of misery and miracle, ruin and rebirth.

Meanwhile, the Moon God will quietly vanish from this portion of the world's darkness, like all those before and after, whether they be deities or students or teachers or friends.

But their light, I can assure you, will remain.

MY NEAR-DEATH EXPERIENCE/
ELVIS TRIBUTE

Appendicized

"Why did you say that about Elvis?" I asked my wife, who was standing beside me at Sgt. Floyd's monument.[1] "Just before my surgery."

Stephanie didn't remember saying anything about Elvis before my surgery, which shouldn't have been a surprise since it was more than twenty years ago.

"What I remember," she added, "is that you thought it was the prune kolache."[2]

That was true. That was, in fact, the first thing I recalled telling the elderly doctor at the rural clinic. "This is probably just the prune kolache I ate this morning," I told him, dismissively, because what I really needed to do was get back to trying (and failing) to write my

---

1. Sgt. Charles Floyd (1782–1804), noncommissioned officer in the US Army and quartermaster in the Lewis and Clark Expedition. Due to a burst appendix, he became the only member of the expedition to die en route. His grave, marked by a large white obelisk, is located on top of a Loess Hill overlooking the Missouri River, near what is now Sioux City in western Iowa. We currently live about ninety miles downstream, in Council Bluffs, Iowa—or "Council-tucky" as my Omaha students sometimes call it. Kentucky is also the home state of Sgt. Floyd. This is the first of several random, seemingly useless associations in this story.

2. Kolache are circular, dense, fruit-centered pastries popular among Czech immigrants and their nostalgic descendants, such as those in the small town where Stephanie

124

dissertation, which was way overdue. The doctor pressed down on my abdomen, released, and a pain shot through my side so intense I actually yelped.

"No, I don't believe this is the kolache," he said and walked over to a large wall poster portraying the human digestive track, placing his finger on it. "I think it's your appendix."[3]

I had to lean forward to see what he was pointing at. Far from threatening, it looked like a puppy's tail or a child's thumb or a spring worm emerging from the dank soil of the large intestine.[4]

"No one really knows what the appendix does, except cause serious health problems," he added.[5] "To be safe, I want you to see a surgeon immediately. Do you feel well enough to drive?"

The regional hospital was over an hour away, and I drove there in one of those freak March snowstorms that can occur suddenly in Iowa. The snow blew unobstructed across the fields and rural roadways, often blinding me. *Why risk my life for a little indigestion?* I wondered. Aside from the abdominal pain, I didn't have any of the symptoms

---

and I lived at the time, near the Bohemian Hills in eastern Iowa. Traditional fillings include apricot, poppy seed, and prune, the latter being preferred by our elderly neighbor who, in her solitude and nostalgia, regularly made too many of them and passed the extras on to us.

3. The vermiform appendix is a narrow, dead-end tube, or diverticulum, extending from the first part of the colon. When its small opening is obstructed, the appendix can become inflamed and rupture, spreading bacteria that can cause a dangerous abdominal infection called peritonitis.

4. The Latin root for vermiform does, in fact, mean "worm-like."

5. There are plenty of theories, however. In our primate ancestors, the appendix may have contributed to the digestion of plant matter—some version of it is found in all the hominoid apes today, including the chimpanzee and orangutan. It has thus been portrayed as a kind of biologically based moral judgment, a "good organ gone bad" from the sins of the modern diet. What was essential for digesting leaves and grass has proven less successful with the Big Mac. Other scientists think it may have assisted our ancestors with digestive tract immunity, a receptacle of "good" intestinal bacteria that, centuries ago, would help repopulate depleted digestive systems after the inevitable, colon-blowing illness. Since it contains immune-cell-producing tissues, some believe it may still play a role in fighting digestive tract diseases. None of these theories has been proven definitively.

listed by the clinic doctor: fever, nausea, vomiting, lack of appetite. I was a twenty-eight-year-old grad student in peak health.[6] The doctor wanted to play it safe, he said, but was this safe? As the car crawled through the increasingly violent storm, I cursed myself for eating all those pastries, still not believing I was destined for the knife.

"Believe it," the surgeon pronounced after a quick examination. "What's worse, I think your appendix is retrocecal, which means the little devil is hiding behind the intestine."[7] His prominent eyebrows lowered, as if steeling himself for battle with an ancient, sentient adversary. "Yes. That would explain the minimal symptoms and the rebound pain—they're tricky that way. And dangerous. Unfortunately for you, this means we can't go low-invasive; I'm going to have to open you up for a little search and destroy.[8] Nurse Heinrichs, are there any interns around who want to see some old-fashioned gut surgery? Well, call them in and get this young man a phone; he'll want to contact family."

I called Stephanie at the rural school where she was teaching and supporting me through grad school.[9] She got on the phone just as they were sticking the IV in my hand and placing my clothes in a plastic bag, like they do for traffic fatalities.

6. Not really in peak health—I was lying around a lot, eating prune kolache, instead of writing my dissertation. But this is what I told myself at the time.

7. What's important to note is that this condition was going to require the surgeon to actually reach into my abdomen and move my intestines in order to locate the offending organ.

8. This regional hospital was apparently well-known for its low-invasive, laparoscopic surgical techniques—"pioneering" is the word I think they used in the promotional materials. This involves making a couple of small incisions into which narrow tools can be inserted to remove the appendix. The wounds are so minor they can be glued shut, effectively eliminating scars that require any future reinterpretation.

9. Stephanie was getting a little impatient with that role at the time. Just prior to the events described, she came home from work to find me lying on the couch in my underwear and watching an all-day *Andy Griffith Show* marathon, which I described as "research." The next morning, while I was still asleep, she detached the television cable and took it with her to school, promising to hold it hostage until I finished at least one goddamned chapter of my dissertation.

"I'm not sure about this," I told her. "I ate a lot of those prune kolache, so maybe I should get a second opinion. This guy seems a little eager."

And that's when she said it.

"Don't risk it. That's how Elvis died."[10]

"What? Elvis didn't die because of his appendix." These were my final words before the surgical nurse took the phone away and let me ride the unspoken question into nothingness: *Why Elvis?*

■

During the intervening decades, Stephanie has been unable to answer that question to my satisfaction. Not that I've asked very often. Come to think of it, this may have been the first time, standing there at the base of Sgt. Floyd's monument. That's another mystery, the reasons why I felt compelled to return to his gravesite for the second time, after ten years. But here on the verge of turning fifty, there's probably nothing I covet more than a little mystery—too many questions have been answered in my life, and in the life of our species. The appendix is not one of them. Its purpose is still unknown, its destiny unclear.[11]

Which is how I like to think of myself sometimes.

A little context. The day I asked my wife about Elvis at the base of

10. I should probably just get this out of the way right now: on the afternoon of August 16, 1977, Elvis Presley, aged forty-two, was discovered unresponsive on the bathroom floor of his Graceland mansion in Memphis, and pronounced dead at 3:30 p.m. Indications are that he suffered a massive coronary that may or may not have been the result of poor health habits, including obesity and over-use of prescribed medications. Not appendicitis. What I believed at the time of my surgery, however, along with many other people, was that The King had perished straining on the toilet, and that his straining had something to do with consuming too much peanut butter—a fate that, given my own long-term abuse of peanut butter, had occasionally given me pause.

11. Some scientists theorize that the appendix is a "maladaptive" organ that hinders our survivability, which evolution is in the process of eliminating. The appendix shrinks in size from childhood to adulthood, and some are born without one at all, suggesting that, like the piggy toe, it may be on its way out. The biological word for this is "vestigial" and, as such, the appendix is often listed alongside human tailbones, ear-wiggling muscles, fetal fur, and goose bumps. But to lump it in with that tame gang of evolutionary blue-hairs is to grossly underestimate its power.

Sgt. Floyd's monument, I had that very morning been gazing at my shirtless self in the mirror, studying the fully exposed scar. Its visibility was somewhat of a triumphant moment, the result of many painful hours at the gym(s), but no one else would have appreciated it as such.[12] Over the years I have secretly obsessed about that scar, which is indeed large, just as the good doctor promised: nearly five inches, whitish and bullocky, like a string of hills on an otherwise flat landscape. There have been many times, standing shirtless in front of that same mirror, when I have been unable to see it tucked beneath the lower crease of my bulging belly, accessible only to touch, a message in braille all too easily transcribed: *get your shit together.*

But now that the scar has reemerged into the light, I'm not sure of its easy meaning anymore. Instead of a landscape or a judgment in braille, it may be some kind of message in a bottle, newly washed up on shore, or beads on a prayer chain, or maybe a trail of hardened breadcrumbs leading me back to some lost source. Or just a hidden wound like any other we carry with us until, suddenly, it becomes visible and demands reinterpretation.

I suppose that begins with the original act of surgical articulation. Or rather, exploration. When the surgeon made the first incision, he was entering a landscape that had never been exposed to light, and yet one illuminated by stories and questions, by meaning, that pre-existed

---

12. With the exception of Stephanie, who definitely appreciates the effort I've put into exercising over the last decade, because I've complained about it constantly. Also, by "gym(s)" I'm referring, first, to the cheap weight bench I set up and used in our living room until I mismanaged the transfer of weights and sent the bar toppling through the glass top of our coffee table. Second, I refer to the "community weight room and cardiovascular area" at the nearby Iowa School for the Deaf. I stopped going there because (since the seventh grade) large groups of teenagers make me nervous and because I didn't know sign language. Together, they made my workout feel, psychologically, like I was running naked through a foreign high school. My third and current gym, Planet Fitness, took over the space previously occupied (in our mostly gutted shopping mall) by a Barnes & Noble bookstore. My favorite treadmill occupies the space where the "Last Chance" bargain book bin used to be, which I avoided after discovering one of my books there. Now I believe the residual fear and resentment hovering in that area may inspire higher aerobic thresholds.

us both. What did I personally know of the appendix at the time? Virtually nothing. In the mid 1990s, during the exploding popularity of what my writing professor called "memoirs of malady"—on depression, addiction, cancer, neuromuscular disease, spanking—I had encountered *nada* by appendicitis victims. Within Western literature as a whole, the appendix had apparently failed to accumulate the privileged symbolic value associated with other body parts—none of the patriarchal power of the phallus or the courage of the spleen or the vulnerability of the heart—though I had seen it mentioned from time to time. I knew, for instance, that the Sylvia Plath poem, "Tulips," was written while she was recovering from appendicitis, and that Willa Cather used the appendix to kill off a major character in my favorite novel by her, *O Pioneers!* [13] [14] [15]

What the surgeon knew at the time, I can only guess, but I know now that the surgery itself was a relatively new answer to an old riddle.

13. In 1916, Nebraskan Willa Cather, a one-time serious student of biology, published her novel, *O Pioneers!*, in which the death of a young and newly married (like me) farmer, Amadee, from a burst appendix inspires his best friend, Emil, to no longer delay consummating his love for a local married woman. Shortly after, the two lovers are shot to death by her jealous husband beneath a mulberry tree. On his way to his doom, Emil rides past the grave of his friend: "That, too, was beautiful, that simple doorway into forgetfulness." This irony is a major reason the book remains a favorite of mine: in a story about conquering prairie wildness, it is the wildness of the body that inflicts the final tragedy on the conquerors.

14. Here's another literary tidbit involving the appendix and a gun: the beloved children's character, Madeline, sports an appendectomy scar that scholar Mary Galbraith argues is symbolic of the author Bemelman's traumatic youth, during which, he claimed, he shot a man in the abdomen.

15. And another: in a novel I was reading only last week, *Beautiful Ruins* by Jess Walter, which is about the emotional damage left in the wake of once relevant, now vestigial Hollywood movie people, a character is writing a thinly disguised autobiography about the death of a soldier friend in WWII: "Sadly, Richards never got to give the Luger to his boy, because six days before we shipped home, me to listen to Cubs games on the radio, him to his wife and son, Richards died ingloriously of a blood infection he acquired in a field hospital, after surgery for a ruptured appendix." The term "ingloriously" captures perfectly a favored literary use of appendicitis, which, although not quite *deus ex machina*, is a convenient choice for deaths that require no explanation beyond basic fact and/or deaths intended to emphasize the meaninglessness of individual hopes and dreams.

I know this because during the intervening decades, I've obsessively accumulated random bits of research on the subject, which I keep in a brown, overstuffed accordion folder located on top of the basement beer fridge—which has itself been linked to the fluctuating health of my gut. In that accordion folder, you will discover that ancient Egyptians made note of the appendix while preparing bodies for mummification;[16] and that in 1492 (a year largely known for other discoveries), Leonardo da Vinci produced the first-known drawings of the appendix;[17] and that the first anatomical descriptions of the appendix didn't occur until 1521; and that in 1886, a Harvard anatomy professor named Reginald Fitz first declared at a meeting of the Association of American Physicians that "appendicitis" (a term he coined) was a distinct and dangerous pathological entity requiring surgery.[18] You'll also find accounts of a surprisingly recent theological debate concerning the appendix.[19]

16. They also referred to it as the "worm" of the bowel.

17. Da Vinci theorized that the appendix was "capable of contracting and dilating so that excessive wind does not rupture the caecum." Literally, a gas bag.

18. Professor Fitz's declaration is perhaps one of the most significant and under-appreciated moments in human medical history, hearkening in "the appendix era," as physician Seldom B. Overlock declared it in his 1928 address to the Connecticut State Medical Society. In that address, Dr. Overlock, much like a retired general lining up orange pips on the tablecloth, described an epic battle to conquer this deadly condition, one hampered by fighting among the ranks (internists vs. surgeons), disastrous campaigns (the use of glass drainage tubes), bad intelligence (surgery used as a last resort only), and senseless sacrifice of the enemy, wrongfully blamed (as with my wife and Elvis) for suffering caused by "over-eating, eating too rapidly, or subsisting on some recommended diet." Most of the heroes of this battle are not generally well-known, but some remain famous due to other accomplishments. These include James Parkinson, who presented the first scientific article on a diseased appendix in 1812, but is best known for first describing the neuromuscular disease that now bears his name. Sir Frederick Treves, celebrated as the "Elephant Man's" surgeon, lost his daughter to a ruptured appendix and later helped establish surgical treatments for the condition. In 1902, Treves operated on England's Edward VII for a burst appendix with abscess the day before he was scheduled to become king, delaying his coronation and, more than likely, his death.

19. The debate centers on whether or not the appendix is one of God's major fuck-ups. Did He or did He not knowingly plant the equivalent of a dirty bomb in our guts, set to go off after a couple million years of evolution? If so, the appendix represents,

From other articles you may glean some appreciation for the countless anonymous individuals who have fallen victim to this entity across
time.[20] Others zero in on a few celebrity victims, and though Elvis is
not among them, Houdini is.[21] And Sgt. Charles Floyd, though I'm
not sure he could be called a celebrity—the story of his life and death
is not well-known, even around here.[22]

––––––

for some Creationists and Intelligent Designers, not just an embarrassing link to our
primate ancestors, but also a serious challenge to the idea of God as perfect (and perfectly benevolent) engineer. One website dedicated to "Things Creationists Hate," lists
the appendix and other "Naughty Vestigial Bits" alongside Charles Darwin, geology,
penicillin, and the Nobel Prize committee. Across the web, you will find a number
of Creationist sites dedicated to disproving the vestigial or maladaptive status of the
appendix, and a number of sites refuting those arguments. The whole thing would
seem ridiculous except that these kinds of "debates" are actually influencing school
boards and politicians representing increasingly vestigial populations like those here
in the agricultural Midwest, who are in turn making decisions severely hindering the
intellectual development of young people and thus our collective chances of survival
beyond the year 2050.

20. It's hard to fathom the numbers, but consider that around three hundred thousand Americans have appendectomies every year, making it the most common emergency surgical procedure of the abdomen, especially among children and teenagers.
Just two hundred years ago, most of these people would have died. Modern surgical
techniques have dramatically reduced the US mortality rates for those with acute appendicitis, but in 1999 (not that long after my surgery) there were still a reported 389
deaths—that's at least one corpse for every day of the year. Globally, in 2013, there were
an estimated seventy-two thousand deaths related to appendicitis, and that's only in
places where such data is collected. These numbers still look pretty good when you
think about how many of our kind have perished from this condition over the centuries.
In short, this sad little worm may be one of the most prolific killers of humanity in the
history of the world.

21. I'd always thought Houdini died during a botched escape trick, chained and
suspended in a vat of water. He actually died of a ruptured appendix, which may or
may not have been caused by two belligerent lads punching him in the stomach prior
to his performance.

22. These are a few of the details I've collected: Charles Floyd was born in 1782 and
spent his boyhood in the wilds of the Kentucky frontier. His family was well respected,
of modest means, and locally extensive, including cousins and grandparents. William
Clark was a family friend, and in 1803, he made the young Army sergeant the first
official appointment to the Corps of Discovery, as quartermaster. Like everyone on
the trip, Floyd was required to keep a detailed journal. About two weeks prior to his
death, while camped along the Missouri River, he wrote "I am very Sick and Has ben
for Somtime but have Recovrd my health again." It is likely Floyd had been suffering
from an infected appendix and that it had ruptured, causing a temporary alleviation of

■

The history, the people, the discoveries, the unanswered questions, the suffering and death, the millions of years of evolution beyond and through our collective consciousness as a species ... I had no appreciation for any of it when I awoke from surgery later that evening. I'd undergone what I thought was, and always had been, a routine procedure. There was no pain, no doubt. The scar, though certainly long, looked tidy and straight, the edges stapled together like the binding of a magazine or the tracks of a toy train. A definitive conclusion. My wrist was attached by tube to an antibiotic drip and a mechanized syringe full of "pain reliever" that I could release with the push of a button—I certainly wouldn't need that. I chatted with Stephanie, watched TV, and went to sleep.

The next morning a nursing assistant tried to walk me, to help jump-start my digestive tract.[23] When I sat up, however, I was overwhelmed by dizziness and nausea. I couldn't stand. The NA insisted I walk, and I insisted I couldn't. Finally, she let me fall back into bed

---

symptoms. Almost simultaneously, on August 3, 1804, the Corps of Discovery had its first meeting with Native Americans, representatives of the Otoe-Missouria tribe, not far from the present-day city of Council Bluffs, an area of Loess Hills and prairies that Floyd found to be "the beautifulest ... I ever saw." During this council, Lewis promised that the US president was someone "from whom you can ask favours, or receive good councils, and he will take care to serve you, & not deceive you." This was an important, if ill-boding moment in American history, and Charles Floyd was alive to witness it. Soon, though, the peritonitis set in, which Lewis mistakenly diagnosed as "Biliose Chorlick" and treated with laxatives—one of the worst things he could have done. Floyd suffered tremendously, but according to Clark's journal, he died on August 20, 1804, "with a great deal of composure." This could not be said of Meriwether Lewis, who would later be appointed governor of Upper Louisiana, but who found his administrative duties to be a distasteful burden that kept him from writing the memoirs of his western journey. He fell out of favor with Jefferson, accumulated serious debt, and never found lasting romantic love. In 1809, near Nashville, Lewis died mysteriously of gunshot wounds, the result of either murder or suicide. He was thirty-five.

23. Another medical mystery. Apparently, though no one really knows why, the bowels (when physically disturbed) work like an old car that needs to be pushed down hill and started in motion. To me, this further confirms the interconnection of all things— we have, in our machines, only replicated our own vulnerabilities.

and left the room.[24] This ritual was repeated in the afternoon, but the nausea and dizziness had worsened to the point where I could barely raise myself off the pillow. The NA didn't seem that concerned; she was preoccupied with readying the room for a new patient, Clyde, a sixtyish stroke victim from the small town of What Cheer, who was wheeled in accompanied by half a dozen family members.[25]

I was annoyed. I certainly hoped Clyde was OK—he wasn't saying anything—but the chatter and sobs and prayers of his relatives were seriously interfering with my ability to hear the television, my only distraction from the increasing abdominal pain. I'd told the nurse about the pain during her last visit, and she'd responded by inserting a catheter, so I wasn't inclined to mention it again.[26] I'd ride it out, with the help of the television, if only Clyde's relatives would shut up.

That evening, Clyde was still sleeping, or comatose, but around midnight he woke up.

"Honey?" he said. "*Honey?!*"

"No one's here, Clyde," I responded. "It's just us."

"Who're you?"

"John."

"I'll be," he said, his voice slow and gravelly. "I haven't seen you since the wedding. Why you married that Phillips girl, I'll never know—she was never any good. We don't talk enough, John. Brothers should talk more than we do."

"I'm not your brother, Clyde."

"Could you get Carolyn? She's waiting for me in the truck and I can't seem to move my legs."

---

24. I would later discover that this NA marked me down in her notes as a "difficult patient."

25. What Cheer, Iowa, is an old coal mining town named by one of its founders after a common English greeting between friends, dating back to the fifteenth century: "What cheer with you?"

26. To be fair, the nurse may have assumed the pain was the result of a bladder infection, which sometimes occurs after abdominal surgery, though her obvious enthusiasm for the procedure may have been inspired by my reputation as a "difficult patient."

"Like I said, Carolyn's not here."

"*Carolyn! Honey!* I'm up here with brother John! Can you believe it?!"

The nurse arrived to calm him down and take his vitals. He seemed to fall asleep, and I was finally on the edge of it myself.

"*Honey?!*"

So it went the rest of our first night together.[27]

Next morning, Clyde's family was once again noisily conversing, but this time I didn't care. The pain had progressed enough that the television no longer served as an adequate distraction; nor did the pain medication, the button for which I'd been working like a video game control. That afternoon, Stephanie's grandfather, Lloyd, dropped by. He was over ninety, and I told him it was very thoughtful of him to drive the hour from his house, where he lived alone.[28] He said he was happy to do it, especially since we were both "appendix survivors"—a designation I suddenly found comforting. Lloyd revealed that, back home in rural Missouri, he had suffered a ruptured appendix around my age and nearly died. "They stuck about five tubes in me to drain the pus out of the abscess," he said. "It would have been one of the worst times of my life, except my first boy, Gary, was born that same week and I had to get out of bed to assist with the delivery."[29] He added

---

27. Stephanie has asked that I clarify her absence here and during the following night. She recalls spending most of both evenings with me, but that she couldn't sleep over because, between the two of us, she had a full-time job and an actual income.

28. Steph had actually lived with Lloyd for six months when she first moved to Iowa in 1990, in order to establish residency and qualify for lower tuition. She remembers their time together fondly, except for the fact that she was working all-night shifts at Hardees during the winter while, fifty miles away, I was enjoying the bohemian life with my grad-school friends. This included a spontaneous bro-trip in my great aunt's 1972 Buick Electra to Mardis Gras in New Orleans during the one weekend in February Stephanie had gotten off work to spend with me. On the way there, I insisted that my buddies and I visit Graceland in Memphis (why?), but the gates were locked.

29. "Gary" is my future father-in-law, who would later voice concern that his future son-in-law had taken a bro-trip to New Orleans, stopping off at Graceland, rather than spending time with his daughter, who had left the rest of her family in Idaho to move to Iowa for the sake of their now tenuous relationship.

that he'd also survived the 1918 flu epidemic, strep, typhoid fever, and cancer at a time when all were poorly treated and mostly fatal.[30]

I asked him how he'd done it and without hesitation he replied, "Faith."

"I don't usually share this story," he continued, "but you're not looking so good and who knows, it might help. One morning, back when I was mining gold in Cripple Creek, Colorado, I was working in a shaft and for some reason I felt sure I was going to die. But then these two figures appeared next to me. They were dressed in glowing white robes, and I just knew they were angels. They didn't speak a word, but somehow they assured me everything would be alright. So don't be afraid, John. There are things in this universe we can't begin to understand."[31]

By the time Stephanie arrived later that evening with my parents, sister, and brother-in-law, the pain had gotten worse; I was feverish and my abdomen appeared to be well into the second trimester of pregnancy. I still hadn't eaten or walked. I must have been moaning or something, because my relatives immediately turned up the volume on the overhead TV, which was showing the Hawkeye basketball game. My mother was an experienced nurse, however, and after taking one look at me, left the room to get help.[32]

"They're paging the surgeon at the Hawkeye game," she said when she returned.

---

30. To give you a sense of just how wimpy Lloyd made me feel, set aside the whole assisting-with-his-son's-birth-with-drainage-tubes-sticking-out-of-his-abdomen thing, and consider that the 1918 flu epidemic alone claimed the lives of fifty to one hundred million people globally, killing over half a million Americans. Regarding typhoid, both he and his sister's husband contracted the illness from some bad cow's milk, and though Lloyd survived, he had to listen to the sounds of his brother-in-law dying in the next bedroom.

31. The appearance of these angels may have been the result of what is commonly called the "Ganzfeld effect," experienced by many miners over the centuries, during which the brain creates hallucinations in response to prolonged sensory deprivation. Then again, Lloyd lived to be ninety-four.

32. She told me later that when she confronted the nurses about my condition, they showed her the notes that labeled me a "difficult patient," to which she responded that the only difficulty she could see was medical negligence.

"They don't need to do that," I replied, annoyed.

"Yes, they do! Your bowels are obviously paralyzed and now you have an obstruction. Whatever you ate before surgery is just sitting there turning to poison and needs to be removed immediately or it could kill you—you already look yellow."

"Kolache."[33]

"What?"

"*Carolyn*, I'm trying to sleep over here! Will you tell brother to please keep quiet!"

Two nurses entered and, as feared, they brought another tube. This time a nasogastric tube the size of a garden hose. They explained that they only had the extra-large tubes and because of the "apparent urgency," they didn't have time to refrigerate it. So this could sting a little.[34] They gave me a cup of cold water and while I swallowed, they jammed the tube up my nose, down my throat, and into my stomach. I vomited green slime all over myself and the bed, which inspired most of my relatives to flee the room.

"He's always had an overly sensitive gag reflex," my mother announced, as if this distinguished me in some way, like royal hemophilia.[35]

The nurses ignored her and watched the attached vessel fill with more green liquid.

33. Technically, the kolache weren't killing me, but rather the resulting infection from the bowel paralysis and obstruction, or ileus, which could have been worsened by any food leftover in my intestines, including the peanut butter sandwich I'd eaten the night before. The lack of walking and the opioid pain reliever I was shooting up may have also contributed. Bottom line, my mother was correct: if it had been left untreated, the bacterial onslaught the appendectomy was intended to prevent could have led to my death.

34. I have yet to find any evidence of the benefits of refrigerating a NG tube before insertion. In fact, the tube, although alleviating some symptoms, does little to cure the underlying infection. This may have been yet another form of torture reserved for those designated "difficult patients."

35. The first time she referred to this gag-sensitivity was at a YMCA camp when I was eight, following a cracker-eating contest in which I nearly choked to death. During this disturbing fireside episode, my mother successfully performed the Heimlich

"Green's not good," one of them said.[36] "We'll need to keep the GI in overnight."

"Carolyn! Please keep them quiet!"

"No," I whispered, the tube scratching the back of my throat. "I don't think I'll be able to sleep with this in."

"Sorry," the nurse replied and left. She returned with a large syringe and then, soon enough, I slept.

When I awoke, everyone was gone, and the room was bathed in the low tangerine of the night-light. The curtain between me and Clyde had been drawn back and we were finally face to face. My mind was foggy, but still hyper-aware of the appendages running out of my body. I was at the bottom of the food chain, lower than the bacteria I was incapable of fighting on my own. Gulliver bound by the Lilliputians. Inside, I remember feeling empty and lost—out of place, out of time. What had these people done to me? What had they taken from my body? Something essential, I was sure, something important enough that my entire digestive tract had paused to grieve. *There are things in the universe we cannot begin to understand.* I worried the appendix might be one of them. If the stories were true, God liked to squirrel away the holy in the most unlikely places: a burning bush, a man's hair, a carpenter's son, a gold mine.

If, as Grandpa Lloyd claimed, angels could be found in that dark shaft, why not the darker, more intimate shafts of the body? What better place to hide the soul?

Granted, I was heavily medicated, and from here I might be tempted to repeat Thomas Huxley's proclamation: "It is not I who

---

maneuver on me in front of a crowd of shocked campers and their families. This memory leads to another interesting piece of medical trivia: the cracker-choking incident occurred in 1975, just one year after Dr. Henry Heimlich published an article on the procedure in *Emergency Medicine*. If it had happened the summer before, who knows where I'd be today.

36. The green color indicates I was vomiting bile, a fluid produced by the liver and kidneys to aid digestion, now pooling behind the kolache/peanut butter dam inside my intestine.

seek to base Man's dignity upon his great toe or insinuate that we are lost if an Ape has a hippocampus minor."[37] But tell that to the man who has lost the ability to create long-term memory because of a stroked-out hippocampus. Or to the younger man who believes that he may die of complications from an appendectomy, as countless have before him. To them, old man, young man, these hidden corners of the body become the literal doorways into forgetfulness, challenging whatever notions they might have had about what is essential, what is meaningful in their bodies—and in their lives.

That's how it was for me, anyway. Whatever questions I had about the purpose of the appendix quickly became subsumed by questions about the purpose of my existence. To what end, if any, had I been created? What had I truly accomplished during my years on this earth? What positive difference had I made? What sins still needed forgiving or remained unrecognized? What was the condition of my soul, if I even had one?

Why go on?

At some point during this existential haze, there was a very loud whistle.

"*C'mere, puppies!*" Clyde again. Another whistle. "*C'mere puppies! Don't just sit there in the grass, John—help me chase down those pups!*"

"What pups?"

"Those Brittany pups over there, in the clearing. They got out of their pen last night. Can't you see them? Momma's going to be sad if we don't round 'em up. Don't let 'em get away, John! *Here, here puppies!*"

---

37. Thomas Henry Huxley (1825–1895), the subject of yet another article in the accordion folder on the basement fridge. In 1861 England, Huxley got in a very public debate with fellow anatomist Richard Owen (1804–1892), an anti-Darwinist who claimed that the hippocampus minor was unique to the human brain, and thus the likely physical location of the soul. Huxley, popularly known as "Darwin's bulldog," vigorously—and correctly—refuted that claim.

"I can't see them, Clyde," I said, but then, after I don't know how long, I thought I could see them, those Brittany pups, running away from us, through the grass. I wanted to chase after them and bring them back home, where they'd be safe. I shouted, "C'mere puppies!" and then Clyde started crying, long whimpering sobs. Then I started crying.[38] Then the crying triggered my overly sensitive gag reflex, causing me to lunge forward into an extended, screaming hack that stunned Clyde into silence. The spell was broken, for both of us, and in a way I was thankful for it.

The nurse entered and I gestured violently that I wanted the tube removed. "I need to walk," I told her, but what I think I was really saying was that I needed to grow up, to elevate myself above the weepy, microbial cesspool I'd become, returning to the superior end of twenty-eight or even two hundred thousand years. She was hesitant at first, but eventually called the surgeon (out of bed this time), who approved the procedure. The walking may help, the nurse told me as she pulled out the tube, triggering another screaming hack, but warned that it would have to be replaced if peristalsis didn't kick in.

So I walked and I walked, though it was painful and nauseating and I had to be accompanied by a pimply nursing assistant who, I knew, just wanted to get back to her murder mystery.[39] But I was going to

38. An editor once told me I cry too much in my nonfiction, which is probably true, and I've only become weepier with age—a fact my sons find endlessly fascinating. It doesn't take much: the image of a baby animal, a commercial for St. Jude's, the sound of my own voice. In this case, Clyde's babbling may have caused some kind of mutual hallucination, tapping into my childhood memories of Brittany spaniels. My first puppy, Flicka, was a Brittany, but she was hit by a car just outside our house when I was five—my first real experience with death. Our next dog was Flicka's sister, Chrissy, and she had a litter of pups sired (intentionally) by a freakishly huge neighbor Brittany named Duke. My first grade teacher, Mrs. Gaedke, normally quite strict, walked the whole class over from Duncombe Elementary to see those puppies, which made me proud and happy, but also afraid of losing them, like the first, which may be why I was crying here. I don't know.

39. I knew this because I had been employed as a part-time nursing assistant just a few years earlier. During one summer of working the night shift, I'd read over a dozen murder mystery novels, including the New Testament.

kick-start this system, I swore, and then turn my life around, treat my body better, my loved ones, live with conviction. I was going to travel the world, write bestselling but honorable books, convert the masses, and alter the dark destiny of our species. *I would rise!*

Then I fainted.

The next morning, I awoke to an icy stethoscope on my belly.

"Nothing," the nurse said. "I'll give it another hour and then I'll have to call the surgeon. More may have to be done. You understand?"

I didn't reply, because I didn't understand. Why was I there? Why wasn't any of it working?

"*Carolyn!*"

"I'm here, Clyde." This time she really was.

"Do you want to watch TV?" the nurse asked me.

I nodded, and she handed me the remote. I was flipping through the channels, finding nothing close to a distraction from the pain, or the despair, when Carolyn peeked her head around the closed curtain.

"I'm sorry to disturb you," she said. I paused on a channel showing some kind of biography of Elvis, which momentarily piqued my interest. Elvis had died on the toilet, I thought, straining to take a crap—something I thought I might never achieve on my own again.

"Sorry to disturb you," she repeated. I didn't look at her. "I was about to say a prayer with Clyde and was hoping you'd permit me to say a prayer for you, as well. I understand you've had a hard time."

"Uh...sure."

"Thank you," she said and retreated behind the curtain just as footage of Elvis singing, live, began rolling on the screen. I can't remember the song, only that he was well into his Vegas years, nearing the end, sweating profusely, his belly straining against the white, sequined jump-suit.[40] I was suddenly very tired. As I slipped back into sleep, I

---

40. The footage may have been from his last televised concert, held in Omaha on June 19, 1977, in the same arena—now gone—where, in 1984, I attended my first concert: The Cars, with opening act Wang Chung ("Everybody Have Fun Tonight"). I went to the concert with my then girlfriend from Shenandoah, Iowa, hometown of the Everly

vaguely remember hearing the sound of Carolyn's prayer mixing with the steady beat of a drum and electric guitar and Elvis's soulful, pleading voice.

I was awakened an hour or so later by another cold stethoscope.

"Whaddya know," the nurse said. "Your bowels are working again. Congratulations."

This was welcome news, for sure, but I couldn't quite wrap my mind around it. Did the walking pay off? All those promises? Or was it something else—Carolyn's prayer or the Elvis song I fell asleep to or perhaps the intertwining of the two overly familiar rhythms, awakening something similar in my gut? An accident?

I didn't spend much time contemplating the answers. Several days later, I was healthy enough to leave the hospital. I said goodbye to Clyde who, like me, seemed to have recovered something of himself. After being regularly corrected by Carolyn, he'd finally accepted I was not his brother. I was a stranger, which meant no more tearful childhood reminiscences, only cautious midwestern conversations about sports, family, work, and weather. During one of his frequent naps, Carolyn told me that if all went well, Clyde would be discharged in a week, though he faced a long road of physical therapy. She wanted us to keep in touch, and I agreed, though I knew we wouldn't. The curtain had once again been drawn between us.

■

In the months that followed, I did my best to keep the promises I'd made in the hospital. I purchased a pair of burgundy sweatpants and took up jogging gravel roads in the early morning. I finished my dissertation, published some essays about the endangered prairies, and

---

Brothers ("Wake Up Little Suzie"), after watching a horse race and drinking cheap beer illegally at Omaha's AK-SAR-BEN Racetrack. The racetrack was later demolished to make room for my university's new campus town, where I now occasionally eat Thai food and sip local craft brew. It is also the location of the new Maverick hockey arena, where my teenage son, Ben, and I attended a speech by President Barack Obama, and afterward talked about our hopes and dreams.

eventually landed a university job in Omaha. We bought an old house just across the Iowa border, here in Council Bluffs, at the top of a Loess Hill, where at night from our bedroom we can see the cluster of Vegas-style casinos on the Missouri River.[41] Stephanie and I have become parents to three boys, two of whom are now teenagers, and we are raising them in this house on a hill, not that far from the hill where Lewis and Clark met with the Otoe-Missouria, and an hour or so downstream from the hill where Sgt. Floyd is buried.

I first visited Floyd's gravesite in 2006, twelve years after my surgery. I went there presumably to research a graduate class I planned to teach on midwestern history and literature, but there were other, seemingly unrelated concerns that may have inspired the need to get away for a while.[42] Heading up I-29, I spotted the monument almost a mile off; once a simple dirt grave marked with a cedar post, it was now marked by a giant sandstone obelisk or "shaft," as it is described on the attached brass plaque. Standing at the base of that shaft for the first time, at the crest of a two-hundred-foot-high Loess Hill, I could appreciate why Floyd's more famous companions had chosen that spot for

41. The house was built in the 1880s, originally a mansion located on land once owned by the family of General Grenville Dodge (friend of Lincoln and builder of the transcontinental railroad), but half of it burned down in 1920. According to the previous owner, now deceased, the house is haunted by the ghost of an asthmatic who committed suicide who she sometimes heard wheezing up and down the stairs. We have yet to hear any wheezing, which is a relief, since I'd hate to think our various medical maladies and scars follow us beyond the grave. Regarding the Council Bluffs casinos, the theme song for one of them is "Everybody Have Fun Tonight" by Wang Chung.

42. These included the usual tripe related to my then upcoming fortieth birthday, but also a stress-related "cardiac event" I had suffered that March, which I think was due to work-related pressures and perhaps to an unhealthy, guilt-ridden obsession with the American wars in the Middle East and to an equally unhealthy, guilt-ridden obsession with the ongoing destruction of the "useless" Loess Hills, some of which were being gutted (or removed altogether) for landfill and construction. In addition, my ninety-two-year-old grandmother, with whom I was very close, announced that same March that she was going off her medications, so she could die on her own terms (was she being "difficult"?). She would pass away only a few weeks after that first visit to Floyd's grave in 2006. She was the last of my grandparents, the last to see me the way a grandparent does: perfect, unspoiled, indispensable. Innocent.

his grave. The view had changed, but it was still impressive, reaching for miles over the interstate, following the river as it fades northwest into primeval green.

Now here I was again, ten years later, in 2016, admiring that same view with Stephanie, carrying some of the same concerns. Except this time I was also obsessing about Elvis.

Why?

"I don't know," Stephanie replied—had I accidentally spoken aloud? "Maybe I just had Elvis on the brain. Wasn't that around the time of the stamp controversy? Young, sexy Elvis versus old, bloated Elvis?"

"He was *only* forty or so," I said, but she was right about the stamp thing—I'd forgotten. A few years before my surgery, and only a few months before Stephanie and I got married, the US Postal Service announced that it would be releasing a commemorative Elvis stamp. They unveiled two designs, one featuring the youthful Elvis purring into a shiny chrome microphone, and another featuring the "mature" Vegas-era Elvis in his white, star-spangled jumpsuit, and asked the public to vote.[43] I vaguely recalled entering a post office somewhere, noticing the large display, and casting my vote for ... *Vegas Elvis!*

It was one of those throwaway, seemingly unimportant experiences, soon forgotten as the day and the life moved on. But now it had

---

43. The Smithsonian National Postal Museum website, under the title "The Elvis Stamp: America Elects a King," describes it this way: "In 1992, the American public voted on a matter of vital national importance: young Elvis or old Elvis?... Pre-addressed ballots were distributed in post offices around the country and in the April 13, 1992, edition of *People* magazine, America spoke, returning nearly 1.2 million ballots to the Postal Service, and the choice was clear: more than 75 percent of voters preferred young Elvis. The stamp was dedicated at Graceland just a few moments after midnight on January 8, 1993—Elvis's 58th birthday. Around the country, reaction to the voting process was boisterous and opinionated. Members of Congress debated the worthiness of Elvis as a stamp subject, newspaper editorialists made lofty pronouncements, and presidential candidate Bill Clinton publicly voiced his support for the younger Elvis. Meanwhile, comedians and cartoonists used the opportunity to poke fun at the Postal Service, the 1992 presidential candidates, and even Elvis himself. A decade later, the Elvis stamp is still one of the most talked-about stamps ever issued by the Postal Service—and the most popular US commemorative stamp of all time."

returned to me, more than twenty years later, on the top of that hill and—how to describe this?—it was as if, in the recovery, the broken pieces of some internal piping were realigned, letting loose an almost overwhelming flood of positive energy and emotion that made me catch my breath for a second and, yes, caused my eyes to well-up.

What had just happened? Why did it matter—*does* it matter?[44]

---

44. Does it matter, for instance, that I was drawn back to Floyd's gravesite, back to memories of my appendix surgery, when I was once again struggling (and failing) to write while seriously questioning the purpose of my existence? Does it matter that when I visited that post office where I voted for Vegas Elvis, it is likely I went there to mail wedding invitations or an early essay manuscript, or both, long before any books were published or children born, or even seemed possible, when all those scary-good feelings of anticipation—about the writing, the life—were intertwined and running through me? Does it matter that the image of Vegas Elvis, the image I voted for in that post office, the image I saw floating on the screen in the hospital before I fell asleep and everything started working again, instantly returns me to the summer of his death, 1977, the summer also of *Star Wars* and *Close Encounters of the Third Kind* and a corresponding light-year expansion of my imaginative life? Does it matter that I saw *Star Wars* for the first time that summer with my two younger cousins, Stephen and David (because I, too, had a locally extensive family), and that when I think of them, I also think of the basement of our grandparents' apartment, where we would often retreat with our action figures and sketch pads to draw out that imaginative life, perhaps on my grandfather's old oak desk, which is now my desk, surrounded by wall-to-wall shelves loaded with knick-knacks and antiques belonging to long-dead ancestors or to his early days as a Piggly Wiggly grocery clerk or to his time in the Army (including a real bayonet and a medicine kit full of mysterious powder) and decorative whiskey bottles in the shape of pirates and wild animals and locomotives and famous monuments, still full of liquor because he didn't drink—all of it, each piece, linked to stories and memories he held close and sometimes told us, most of which are now lost? Does it matter that when supper time arrived, we would walk up those basement stairs to find our grandparents, whom we loved and who loved us, sitting in their respective recliners, chatting and watching the news on their cabinet television, which, during that late summer of 1977, the season also of Sgt. Floyd's passing, ran many images of Vegas Elvis, whose death didn't seem like an ending to me but part of a beginning, my beginning, and his, because I'd never really known Elvis until then, when he first came alive in my imagination alongside Luke Skywalker and the spaceships in *Close Encounters* that flashed and sparkled like the sequins on his Vegas jumpsuit? Does it matter that in the small living room of that apartment, where my grandparents and my cousins and I watched those Elvis tributes, the colors of the shag carpet and furniture and curtains and crocheted throw pillows and the God's-eye wall hanging—olive green, brown, orange, burgundy—made it seem forever late summer, retaining the heavy, contemplative warmth of that season in Iowa, even during the cold months to come? And does it matter that when I drive by that apartment today, on my way to visit my parents, now the grandparents,

Whatever it was, it was now gone.[45]

"OK, OK," Stephanie said, "but what about Sgt. Floyd? What's the connection, besides the appendicitis?"

"I don't know," I said, and I didn't. Like the scar on my abdomen, like the Elvis thing, Floyd had become yet another nagging mystery, another bottled message on the beach, another trail of breadcrumbs leading ... where? I recalled touring a museum in nearby Sioux City during that first trip in 2006, where I'd read the informational displays on the Corps of Discovery, most of them dedicated to Thomas Jefferson, Lewis and Clark, and the native tribes they encountered— including the "medals of friendship" that now represent all the broken promises made to them by our government.[46]

I always assume the door will be open, even though strangers live there, because it was one of the few places where I never had to knock, and where, without question or doubt, I always felt welcome?

45. Was it gone? There is part of me that still feels the warmth of that apartment, that year, even as I write this (I've been writing a lot again, thankfully), sitting at an oak desk in a basement room where the wall-to-wall bookshelves are loaded with knick-knacks and antiques and decorative whiskey bottles inherited from my grandfather. It is a place where three boys have come to draw and play, including with my *Star Wars* action figures, and to ask about the ancient artifacts on the shelves, such as the knife collection my grandfather gave me for Christmas in, yes, 1977. Perhaps Günter Grass was onto something when he wrote of 1977, which included for his narrator a weird obsession with Charlie Chaplin (the Elvis of his time?): "These things leave their mark." Consider my cousins Stephen and David, both of them fathers approaching fifty who have similar rooms in their houses, displaying similar items inherited from our grandfather. Recently, I learned that Stephen has petitioned his wife to redecorate their basement in shag carpeting and furniture of a style and color reminiscent of a late summer in 1977. Does she understand what is at stake in such a request?

46. The Otoe and Missouria tribes, the first to whom these medals were given, were farmer-hunters who had settlements near the Missouri and Platte Rivers. By the time they officially met with the Corps of Discovery in the summer of 1804, both tribes had been decimated by smallpox, leading them to combine their populations, which numbered around 250. Not long after that historic meeting at the council bluff, conflicts arose between the Otoe-Missouria people and the increasing influx of white settlers who attacked them, violated treaties, and stole their land. In 1855, despite the late Meriwether Lewis's assurances that the US government would "take care to serve you, & not deceive you," that same government forcibly confined the tribe to a reservation in southeast Nebraska, where they suffered from illness and starvation, losing many children. In 1881, they were moved once again to Red Rock, Oklahoma, and their

Floyd did get some decent attention at the museum, thanks to the proximity of his grave. I read his journal entries describing the "Butifulest" prairie hills where we have both, in our own ways, settled, and about his painful death from a ruptured appendix, the fate we might have shared. I also read about a letter he dictated just before he died. "I am going away," he said to Clark. "I want you to write me a letter." What was in that letter, or if it survived, is one of the lingering mysteries of that historic journey, though it has largely been subsumed by the dramatic adventures and discoveries that followed.

Since then, Sgt. Floyd has been reburied three times due to scavenging animals, the shifting Missouri River, and finally to inter him at the bottom of the sandstone shaft that, as one poet wrote, is "like a finger, pointing high."[47]

Floyd's great-great-niece, a forensic anthropologist, used a mold of his skull to recover his likeness, which was mounted in the museum, dressed in uniform complete with musket, before a panorama of the land as it was then, wild and virtually uncharted. As I stood before him in 2006, on the verge of turning forty, his face impressed me as deer-like, curious and tragic. The one left behind. The one cut short, needlessly, by a maladaptive, vestigial link to an ancient self. I thought of all that had transpired without him in the history of that journey, his family, these hills, this nation, our species. All that could have been. I felt it in my gut, still feel it, the ache for the missing parts, the lost possibilities—how do we commemorate them?

---

children were sent away to government schools where they were forced to abandon their language and culture, deemed useless (and dangerous) to American society. The Dawes Act, passed in 1887 by the US Government, was then used to acquire and redistribute tribal land to private owners, sparking a legal battle that lasted until the 1960s. Currently the combined Otoe-Missouria tribe includes around three thousand members, most of whom reside in Oklahoma, where, as their website says, "they have parlayed their gaming revenue into long-term investment in sustainable industries including retail ventures, loan companies, agriculture, natural resource development, hospitality, entertainment and several other projects still in development."

47. Which finger?

Feeling sorry, I suppose, and I did feel sorry for Charles Floyd. Only twenty-two, just six years younger than I was when I went under the knife for the same malady. There was all that could have been, all that I have seen of life that he did not. But later that day, when I returned to his burial site after visiting the museum, stepping into the warming air, into the glare of that tall, pale shaft, what I mostly felt was envy. It may not be such a bad thing, I thought then, to have missed the rest of the story. To be forever at peace in a land you found new and beautiful and full of promise.

Ten years later, however, in 2016, on the verge of turning fifty, standing in that same spot with Stephanie, admiring that same view of the Missouri River, the still-beautiful, fragile hills, I wasn't as interested in feeling sorry or envious. I wasn't as interested in what had been lost. I was interested in what had been saved—not just out there, but in here. In him. In that deathbed letter—*what was in it?* That mattered a lot to me, suddenly. In the middle of his tremendous suffering, on the edge of oblivion, what had been called forth from the margins of his life and memory, and put into words? Had it helped in any way to transform that suffering into what Clark described as "composure"? Had it transported him, as Clyde and I had been transported all those years ago, and me just a few minutes prior, to a time, seemingly vestigial, when he had been among people and places he had loved and thought lost?

Here was another throwaway moment, quickly discarded as Stephanie and I made our way back down from the grave and drove the long miles home to Council Bluffs, where our children were waiting for us, in the world as it is. Their world. Now, though, writing these words in my basement room, at the top of another Loess Hill, in yet another underground place of commemoration, it seems to me the question may represent one of the saving curiosities of age. What else has been accumulated from the growing appendices of my life, and from the life of our maladaptive, terminally ill species, to horde in secret until all else erodes or is forgotten or wasted away? Until a seemingly final moment—*are we there yet?*—when, at last, it must be revealed and spent.

More suffering, possibly, and fear and regret and sin, the scars we have projected onto the world and those who will inherit it. Or will something unexpected emerge that might yet remind us of our embodied existence as loved and cherished animals—if not by God, then by at least a few of our kind and by the planet itself? Something that will not only bring composure to our eventual, collective passing and to that of the beautifulest places, but delay that passing indefinitely. New and healthier promises, new possibilities for redemption that will rip aside the false curtains separating us as strangers.

Inside such an awareness, what might we discover?

Perhaps the answers to all the mysteries we have longed to solve, the maps to all the frontiers we have hoped to explore.

Or something less ambitious, but equally useful. Like a puppy or a worm or a song.[48]

---

48. Or even a soul.

MY BREAK-UP LETTER

Dear America

May 18, 2017

Dear America,

I've come here to one of my favorite spots of Nebraska prairie to think over our relationship, and I've come to a decision: I love you, but I need some time off.

No, this isn't because of the argument we had last night in bed.

Not that you would have noticed, but these last few months since the election have taken a huge toll on me emotionally. I haven't been sleeping well and that little tremor in my eyelid has started up again. I've been spending a lot more time in the basement, and less time out here, where I belong—where *we* belong.

Yes, I know we've been together for fifty years, and, yes, I know we have had some amazing times together. Like last spring on that beach in Malibu when we found the exact spot where, in *The Planet of the Apes*, Charlton Heston got down on his knees in front of a nuclear-decimated Statue of Liberty and screamed "Damn you all to HELL!"

OK, maybe that's not the best example, but still, I think every relationship can benefit from a little time off now and then. Maybe it will give us the space we need to truly reflect on why our relationship, our *love*, matters. Before it's too late.

I realize the problem isn't just you, America. I've taken our relationship for granted, I admit it. I've been complacent and weak; I've stayed silent when I should have spoken up, which I think you may have mistaken for unconditional support. My country, right or wrong.

But in my defense, there have been times when your behavior has left me completely speechless. Three years ago, for instance, in 2014, when you knew I was grieving a particularly brutal year of grasslands destruction, with 3.7 million acres lost. You may not think that's a big deal, but since you've become so obsessed with belittling countries south of the border, let me put it this way: that's more than twice the acres the Brazilian Amazon lost to deforestation.

And how did you respond to my feelings that summer? You bought a gold-plated treadmill and started blabbering about making yourself "great again." Can you blame me for thinking that was just a bad joke? And please don't give me that Big-Ag crap about being a good provider. I didn't fall in love with the size of your bushels-per-acre or your checkbook or your ego. I fell in love with your compassionate, democratic, poetic prairie soul!

We used to read actual poetry together, remember? Before you, once again, threatened to defund the NEA? Whitman was our favorite, the guy who called the prairies "America's characteristic landscape," the thing that made it *truly* great—"that vast Something, stretching out on its own unbounded scale, unconfined … combining the real and ideal, and beautiful as dreams." Not to mention all the other passions we once had in common, such as national parks and safe drinking water and feeding poor children and providing medicine for the sick and voting. And facts.

Now I'm just not sure anymore.

I know exactly what you're thinking as you read this: *you don't understand me!* Or worse, you're planning to guilt-trip one of your drinking buddies into leaving me another Facebook message about how you just need "a little more time."

Don't even.

I've been there, done that again and again, but every morning it's the same old crap. I get out of bed, maybe pick a prairie pasqueflower petal (just one, since there's not that many anymore) to put by your plate, make us breakfast, and then you show up and start in on the immigrants, the Muslims, the Wall, the fake news, the fake science, *blah, blah, blah,* and it's like I go invisible and you completely forget the pasqueflower petal and the amazing huevos rancheros sitting right in front of your face.

It's driving me nuts, America!

And then just last week you proposed "reviewing" national monuments to allow development, as well as withdrawing from the Paris Agreement, which you then bragged about at that dinner party we attended. When I tried to talk with you about it during the drive home, you started yelling at me about how I wouldn't disrespect Sweden like this, or Australia or Russia or China or Canada (I can't remember all the nations you mentioned, but it was a lot).

Honestly, do you have any concept of how lethal your stupidity can be?

I'm sorry if I sound angry, America, but guess what: you don't have a monopoly on that emotion. Plus, if there's any chance of us staying together, we're going to have to start being honest with each other. And there's no way around it: I *feel* angry. And betrayed. I mean, I've stood by you during some pretty difficult times. Like twenty-five years ago, when I first discovered how you'd spent the entire century before we met destroying prairie ecosystems, leaving them among the most endangered on the planet, and that you were *still* sneaking off at night to snort "just a few more acres."

I could have left you then, but we talked it out, and even though part of you continued snorting prairie (like during that epic binge in 2014) there is another part of you that joined me in trying to save it.

I will never forget the days we spent together seed collecting and pulling up garlic mustard and trying to boost the spirits of those patriots on the front lines of restoring and protecting the native land that

I know, deep down, you still love. Not to mention all those hot hours in the tall grass right here at Glacier Creek Prairie when, despite the ticks, we couldn't keep our hands off one another. *Pure sweetness!*

But for you it never seemed enough.

You continued to stubbornly cling to your addictions, including all those conjugal visits with Fracking in North Dakota. I tried to convince myself your infatuation with that promiscuous twenty-something industry is understandable, given your age. But then I find out you're back at it full steam with coal! Hasn't that withered old perp done enough damage? You of course denied it all, but when I confronted you with the sordid pictures and research, the ruined lives—those pesky *facts*—you told me to stop getting "triggered," that it was only about the money. Don't be so negative, you said; suck it up and embrace hope. Honestly, the only hope I feel some days is that the catastrophic climate change you are causing will finally melt the moral icicle stuck up your hypocritical ass!

There I go again with the anger, and I swore I wouldn't, for the kids' sake. We haven't talked about the kids, but then again, you haven't spent much time with them recently.

Remember your children?

I'm raising three of them right now, and trust me, if it wasn't for them, I might have given up on you years ago. And no, I haven't told them everything you've been up to—I won't put them in the middle— though sooner or later they're going to figure it out. Despite me taking them to this beautiful prairie and telling them about the many good things you've done, are still doing, I can't prevent them from seeing you on TV and on the internet, throwing the ball around with the polluters and gun idolaters and hate mongers and military drones and anti-vaxxers and the Confederacy (*seriously?*), all of whom are making it less and less safe for their kind to go to school, or even step outside.

They're asking a lot of questions I'm finding hard to answer.

Still, they love you, and it breaks my heart to think of them losing faith in you. In us.

I guess that's ultimately why I'm writing this letter, why I'm asking for a little honesty and a little space. Maybe the space between here and Iceland. Or maybe just between our house and an apartment you rent across town, where we can spend the odd night together; just enough for us to gain a little perspective. To remember why we care. And I *really* need you to care right now, *truly* care, and not just for our children and for our friends and for the prairie, but for every living thing on this planet—because I know you're capable of it.

Because I know, despite everything, your soul is big enough!

Did I just say something hopeful? Maybe it's because I'm sitting here in this fragile 320-acre prairie in the middle of Omaha, which, despite the odds, continues to survive. Could it be the same with our romance?

Well, you know better than anyone what a bleeding-heart softie I am. Sometimes, between the sheets, you've called me your "sweet little buttercup," even though you know perfectly well *Ranunculus acris* is not a native prairie plant. But I guess if we're being completely honest, that's what I'll always be.

As I said, I still love you, America. Desperately.

But let me be clear, if you ever call me "triggered" again, I swear to god I'll kick your tail all the way to Mars.

From what I hear, you're going there anyway.

Affectionately yours,

John Price

MY ARCTIC EROTICA

Fifty Shades of Grímsey

"You are quite the disciplinarian," I hiss.
"Oh, Anastasia, you have no idea."
—*Fifty Shades of Grey*

How could a place so cold be so *hot?*

This is my first thought when I spy the woman across the cabin of the stalwart Icelandic fishing vessel, christened *Saefari*. She is peering through rain-fogged windows at the increasingly aroused, arctic waters. Curly mahogany hair, kissed with grey, splashes upon wool-sweatered shoulders—an exotic beauty! Yet, there is something familiar about her. Perhaps because in some parallel world, or previous life, we have been married twenty-five years and own a house in Iowa and are raising three sons and taking our first vacation alone together in nearly two decades.

Either way, there is an instantaneous draw, an undeniable magnetism that charges the air between us and sets my body and all the bodies about me to swaying, woozily.

Could it be only the waves?

During my approach—*are my feet moving?*—I try, desperately, to reorient. We are on a fishing vessel, I remind myself, which also doubles as a passenger ferry. It departed the northern port of Dalvík this very morn, cruised up the elongated Eyjafjörður, fully engorged by winter snowmelt, and past Siglo village, where herring girls once gutted and salted oil-slick bodies on decrepit piers.

Now we sail upon open and uncertain seas. All to deliver a small group of wayfarers to the island of Grímsey.

And for what reasons?

While others of our kind have chosen different, *hotter* places for such life journeys, we the passengers of the stalwart vessel *Saefari* have chosen to breathe cold fish guts and pound through storm-angered waves to reach a two-mile basalt crag that, in a few thousand years, will likely disappear beneath these same waters. Absorbed by the world's coming fever dream.

Even so, as I approach the event horizon of this alluring human, I taste a sweet (and salty) anticipation in the air. Above my head, over the roar of the engines, I catch fragments of a video narrated by a former captain: "If something happens, I start by giving a warning sound..." and "...what happens tomorrow or how this will end."

Oh my.

I slide into the seat beside her. Dark eyes turn to meet mine, short-circuiting my medulla oblongata, making it difficult to breathe. Lips approach my ear, a whisper: "I think I'm going to barf."

She is gone.

She returns—*an eternity!*—and collapses into the seat. Her hair smells, enticingly, of fish scales and bile. It is a moment of sublime vulnerability and I move quickly, drawing forth the box of Tic Tacs. I shake two tiny, egg-shaped mints into her open and eager palm. I put my arm around her.

She moans.

We are on our way.

■

Grímsey Isle, on the approach, appears grey and dim through the rainy sea mist. *Mysterious.* From the deck, I gradually discern a lighthouse and a church and some houses. The green, treeless land rises behind and above these structures, like a cresting wave or the shoulder of a sleeping lover seen for the first time across the expanse of flannel sheets.

The question is the same: Are we to be swept away or subsumed?

Two dozen of us disembark into the scruffy village of Sandvík, the island's lone and tenuous center of civilization, population ninety-some and decreasing—the children are not returning. No one is there to welcome us. As the legend goes, Grímsey was first settled by a man named Grímur, who was either a bloodthirsty Viking or a lusty farmer or both. He found the place overrun by giants and trolls and slew them, claiming one of their daughters for a wife. I have heard the hardy fishermen here boast direct descendancy.

Another erotic legend: in 1793, the island was nearly abandoned when plague took the lives of most of the men, and the rest were lost while sailing to the mainland for help. Only the women and one man remained, a priest. It is said he helped repopulate the island.

And another, even *hotter*: in the mid-nineteenth century, wealthy journalist and US chess champion, Daniel Willard Fiske, glimpsed the island from a passing steamship and fell in love. He never set foot on its shores, but nevertheless showered the locals with courtship gifts: a school, a library, firewood, loads of money, and a chess set for every farmhouse on the island. Iceland loves chess; he knew this. He must have known, as well, that he was tossing into this isolated, molten stew of troll, Viking, shepherd, and priest one of the most ancient instruments of naked intellectual grappling.

And so, for well over a century, on every Grímsey farmstead, beneath furs and in front of solstice fires, queens have taken rooks have taken bishops have taken pawns. Countless check mates.

A memory returns: Many years ago, there was once a young woman I newly loved—*was she this same stranger?* We used to play chess on the floor of my small room in a college student boarding house, after feasting on Rice-A-Roni and pickled artichoke hearts. We played on a Mexican chessboard made of sparkling green-and-white stone. I cannot recall who won or lost more games, only that it seemed to change every night, and did not matter.

The German woman beside us heaves her insides all over the pier.

"Oh, god, I'm afraid," says my beguiling companion. I take her face in my hands, gently, as if to say, *I am here.*

"No, I'm afraid I'm going to barf again."

I let go of her face.

We do not dawdle. Hand in hand, we walk the coastal trail through a wind-scoured, treeless terrain. We pause before a small private cove. We should keep moving—we have only four hours—but we are entranced by smaller wonders: lichen-kissed volcanic rocks; swollen, frost-billowed bosoms of grass; flesh-beaked Eurasian oystercatchers. Eider ducks float just offshore, in pairs, on waves that undulate and caress the exposed rocks at low tide—far cry from the rough seas only recently traveled.

I am feeling better, she says to no one.

And yet, I observe a touch of green lingering on her cheek, the only flesh visible beneath her full-body rain suit. It is more than enough! Inside roils dreamy nostalgia for the green women of my youth: Marvel's She-Hulk; the emerald queen on that Mexican chess board; and the green woman "Vina"—from Star Trek episodes eleven and twelve, "The Menagerie"—who, with the help of alien mind control, would restore a burned, paralyzed Admiral Pike to happiness and vitality on the forbidden planet Talos IV.

I recall that, somewhere in a place called Iowa, on a basement bookshelf, there is a small toy Vina standing next to the golden-haired Deco brand Thor-with-hammer action figure I got from Santa in 1977, when I was eleven. As on Talos IV, the vision of this menagerie returns me to a place where the mind is no longer chained to earthly infirmities: enlarged prostates and colonoscopies and root canals and high cholesterol and, most perplexing of all, the cooling of desire itself.

I wish, like Thor, I could control the weather.

In the presence of this real-life greenish woman, however, I feel it again, the quickening flame. The gathering lightning. And something else: an intensity I cannot quite decide is pleasure or pain. I dismiss it, not because it is nothing, but because I think it might grow to be unbearable.

Kría!

We spot the arctic tern as it swivels over the water. Its wings are black-edged scimitars slicing through the air. Thousands of them are returning from annual migrations along the coasts of Europe and Africa, Australia, even Antarctica. I am reminded of what little I have seen of the world. By the time this bird dies, it may have traveled 1.5 million miles, a journey to the moon and back nearly three times—among the longest migrations in existence. It has returned to Grímsey to find a lifelong lover, to nest on the ground and raise babies.

Kría!

A warning?

Guidebooks direct visitors to avoid tern nesting grounds. You will be dive bombed, they say, beaks jabbing at your cranium, drawing blood. *Wear a hat!* But my greenish ladylove and I are at a safe distance, as the nesting sites are on the other side of the airport's small runway. With so many terns returning, they can disrupt the descent of small tourist planes, forcing multiple approaches. Emergencies.

■

Soon we reach the spot that is among the main reasons people journey to Grímsey: the invisible, magnetic border of the Arctic Circle. Well-pecked cranium of the globe. Geographical locus of the Seventh Chakra, pathway to the Sacred. Or perhaps the First Chakra, near the base of the spine, connecting us to the ground beneath our bodies— Jǫrð, the ancient Norse called it. Earth physical.

The mantra for this First Chakra, according to my copy of *Meditation for Dummies* is: "I am safe and at home in the world and in my body."

Am I?

There is, of course, a monument—a cylindrical, steel tube suspended between two rock piles marking the boundary of the Circle, over which is a metal platform. A Japanese couple is first in line; they walk up the steps and stand on the platform, on either side of the tube. They giggle and embrace across it for a photo. Above them, at the top of a pole, signs point in different directions: Sydney (16,317 km), Tokyo (8,494 km), New York (4,445 km), Moskva (3,103 km), London (1,949 km), Reykjavik (325 km).

At first, I am disappointed. The monument is small and spare, yet the immensity of its meaning soon raises my repressed body hairs. In the words of Annie Dillard: "This is the end of the Via Negativa, the lightless edge where the slopes of knowledge dwindle, and love for its own sake, lacking an object, begins."

But love must first have its object, so here we are, on the iceless threshold that leads to the sublime place of which Dillard speaks. The place where Polar explorers of old dreamed of finding a realm of simplicity and purity to perform, as she puts it, "clear tasks in uncontaminated lands"—a passageway between worlds. Alas, they did not fully grasp what they and their ships were approaching and died for their ignorance.

Will it one day be said that we, too, were "not sufficiently sensible of conditions"?

At the monument, we certainly do not grasp what it is we are approaching, because (as I will find out later) it is not here. The actual border of the Arctic Circle has shifted north, nearly off the coast. The next fall, the good people of Grímsey will place an eight-ton rolling boulder—*Orbis et Globus*—on that true boundary, consecrated by the flourish of a solo trombone. As the boundary shifts, *Orbis* will follow, maybe into the waters of the Greenland Sea. In a few decades, the borderline will leave the island altogether. Over the next ten to twenty thousand years, it will drift far to the north, where currently there is ice, before returning to this very spot.

What will remain of Grímsey then? What evidence will remain of those, like us, seeking to cross boundaries once believed safe and unchanging? Sacrosanct.

Who will be left to blow the trombone?

The Japanese couple has finally finished, and it is our turn. We approach the stairs as countless others have before us, in a ritual of love that resonates with other such rituals we have perhaps known. Two embodied worlds, on either side of the world, navigating the passage between. We are stepping upward, suspended above *Jǫrð* and the icy depths, to complete the pure task, to take the silent vow: a joining with all that chooses to be joined.

She faces me across the void and removes the hood of her rain parka—a touch of green still on her cheeks. I become shy. She takes my hands.

And then, for what may or may not have been the first time, we kiss.

■

When I awaken, we are sitting near the towering Básavík cliffs, a cacophony of bird-and-wave noises filling the air, our bodies. We are being ravished!

On the rocky ledges, in the air, on the distant waves below are the birds who call this place home, for now. Gulls, guillemots, terns I recognize, others I learn about later: black-legged kittiwake, northern fulmar, razorbill, black guillemot, and murre (both common and thick-billed). Deliciously seductive names. This island is a sexual sanctuary—sixty bird species visit its shores, over half choosing to nest. Birds outnumber humans here ten thousand to one. It is not a place meant for the heat of mammals, which is good, since on similar islands rats and cats are wreaking havoc with seabird populations. Grímsey is mercifully free of such animals, except for the humans and their sheep, which, wingless, rarely go anywhere.

I like birds, but I did not come here for them.

I came, in part, for something I hardly recognize until the moment is upon me, here on the cliffs, in the midst of this indecipherable cacophony: the experience of being *away from* whatever else I am elsewhere. To be story-less, history-less, nation-less. Exotic. Migratory. To experience, as if by magic, what is growing between this seeming stranger and I, alone together, new and renewed, in a pure and uncontaminated land.

I take her in my arms—we are doing it! *Snuggling! Oh god,* how long has it been?! She nestles against my chest, puts her chin on my clavicle, which even beneath the layers sort of hurts, so I adjust, which makes our rain suits *swish,* creating invisible sparks, electrifying the atmosphere—clouds parting, birds screaming, ocean roaring.

Do I hear "The Flower Duet" by Delibes?!

No matter. Inside, I feel it again: the rising intensity. The gathering lightning. The almost unbearable *ecstasy!*

We are being watched.

I turn my head and catch him: a diminutive voyeur, about ten yards away, peeking at us through the grass. And just like that, the snuggling is over—interrupted by a small being, unaware, as has occasionally happened in some other world I vaguely remember. The little creature waddles closer and I recognize him. *Fratercula arctica,* named so by Linnaeus for the black-and-white plumage resembling monastic robes and for the northern constellation of the Great Bear. But this is no bear. The bright orange and red facial colors of this plump, chicken-sized creature resemble its more popular nicknames: "clown of the sea" and "ocean parrot."

Puffin.

I have seen them only in photos and videos and behind glass in an Omaha zoo. Here they are legion—over thirty thousand reside on Grímsey. Most of the puffins on this planet reside in Iceland, with around five million breeding pairs. We shift our position and spot countless numbers of them decorating the black lava cliff sides, like sconces, or in great and colorful slicks upon the waves below.

"Oh, puffins!" she exclaims.

I am momentarily jealous but have to confess these colorful companions grant the dim scene a touch of the theatrical. A splash of sensual cosplay. Of *hotness*.

Indeed, we have apparently arrived in the early dawn of puffin mating season. The fiery colors are their breeding plumage, little candles ignited after many solitary months doused at sea. That is how they winter: alone, on the water, in the dark. They return to Grímsey in the spring—if they return—to seek a mate or to be reunited with the one to whom they have already chosen to be joined, for they are monogamous. It is not known whether they reunite offshore or on land.

Each is a votive, flickering. Lighting the way to adoration!

The first to arrive prepares the old nesting site, to which they both return every year. They nest in burrows dug underground or on cliff sides, both of them doting on the one egg they usually produce per year. They are as loyal to place as to their mates. Specifically, to the cliff sides where they first took flight as pufflings or *pysja*—the "place of liberation" as it is sometimes called. Later, if they're lucky, it will become the place from which their own pufflings take flight.

Is that also, for the parents, a kind of liberation?

Such questions are for later. Now is for the young lovers—and since wild puffins may only live to be twenty, they are always young. And in love.

The ground beneath us seems to growl, as those who have returned to prepare the nest purr and vibrate with anticipation. Nearby, there is a sudden conflagration of noise. Two puffins, fully aflame, approach one another, heads wagging. The closer they come, the louder the noise of the gathering crowd. When the couple finally meets, they rattle their beaks together, pause, then do it again. And again. The crowd roars!

The billing!

Storied mating ritual of the puffin—a playful face spanking that will continue throughout the egg-laying season. It occurs between the newly joined and the long-committed reunited after many treacherous months at sea. Which version we are witnessing here, or anywhere, makes no difference. Either way, there has been an excruciating wait. And now its resolution: this hard, familiar touching, reverberating through the bills, the feathers, deep into the flesh.

Into the earth itself, *Jǫrð*, which growls and purrs.

Unbelievably hot.

■

We continue along the trail, following cliffs high above the ocean's edge. We are still holding hands, like the vaguely familiar nineteen- and twenty-one-year-olds who first met many years ago in a parallel world and played chess. Secret coves, like memories, come into view below us. They don't seem as full as those near the Billing Grounds of Básavík. Perhaps we have contracted a touch of puffin fever, well-known, for it is now that dynamic, colorful creature our eyes exclusively seek—the flickering flames, the love sconces.

We don't spot any puffin in these coves, only gulls, and so we deem them empty.

I am hungry.

Maybe that's why my mind goes gloomy, the low blood sugar— among the infirmities from which I would ask to be liberated by Vina, green woman of Talos IV. I recall reading how along these very cliffs, in starvation times, Grímsey men rappelled to collect eggs. Even now, when no one is starving, the eggs are collected and eaten. Even the once-a-year puffin egg. Even the puffins themselves, especially during the summer hunt, called *lundaveiðer*. Each year on Grímsey, thousands of puffins are harvested, though the IUCN has officially declared them "vulnerable," their global population dramatically decreasing. In Iceland alone they have declined by almost half since 2003.

It is explained that such hunts are, like the birds themselves, part of a dying Nordic tradition, its festivals and feasts going back centuries. Hungry Vikings of old would follow seabirds to new shores, consume them, and thank the gods.

That's one thing, but this is another: I once watched Gordon Ramsey consume, between F-bombs, a puffin meat salad. He compared the taste to liver. He then headed out to the Westmans, the largest puffin colony in Iceland, possibly the world. Using a big triangular net on the end of a pole, called a *háfur*, he snagged the birds mid-flight, like butterflies, only in this case the butterflies cried like lambs before getting their necks snapped.

There are new laws and limitations, but puffin can still be found on Icelandic menus, along with fermented Greenland shark (IUCN "near threatened") and fin whale (IUCN "vulnerable"). The shark, on these menus, is called *hákarl* and the whale is called *hvalur*. Puffin meat is called *lundi*. It is often boiled or smoked ("in the tuxedo") and served with a rich curry sauce to countless tourists in Reykjavic, over countless candlelight dinners.

There are other forms of starvation.

■

The trail turns inland, through the scurvy grass—also consumed in starvation times, as it contains vitamin C and other medicinal properties. The earth beneath this grass undulates with small hillocks. They aren't nests or mammalian diggings, because there are no mammals. They are, I assume, created by the same upheavals that split and ruin asphalt streets in that other, parallel world. The perpetual freezing and thawing of the ground. They look like green loaves of bread.

I am still hungry.

Mercifully, we enter the distraction of a sweetly heated, uninterrupted conversation—something that may or may not be an extreme rarity in that other world of ruined asphalt.

Either way, the thaw is upon me.

It starts slow, with a couple buttons about politics, and then it's like we're in an elevator and verbally tearing each other's rain suits off. Totally intoxicating! Wild! Scratchy! *Hot!* We talk freely of what we have read, what we have thought and believed and hoped and learned

during the last few years. Music! Philosophy! Science! Parallel dimensions! We talk of the Earth, of God, of the divine nature of Love. We
talk of what we might yet do, who we might yet become.

Dreams!

Though I do not say it aloud, I am suddenly reminded of a book I
once read, perhaps shared with me by this same woman in a parallel
dimension. It is the story of two privileged white people living in another rainy, ocean-licking place. The man is a wealthy entrepreneur
with a helicopter who supports ecologically sustainable agriculture. He
wants to cure world hunger. The woman is a college student and part-
time journalist. Deeply in lust, then maybe love, they have—because
of some inner damage—signed a contract permitting one to assume
the role of dominant, the other submissive. To spell out clearly, and
consensually, the rights and regulations of inflicting both pleasure and
pain in a hidden "playroom." The rules for relinquishing control. Or
exercising it.

In doing so, the main character, Anastasia, quotes her favorite novel,
Tess of the d'Urbervilles: "I agree to the conditions, Angel; because you
know best what my punishment ought to be; only—only—don't make
it more than I can bear!"

When the pleasure and pain, the intensity, become too much, they
have a "safety word," though I cannot remember what it is. Only that
I found the whole thing laughable—as did many of my friends. The
novel's popularity was, at best, a curiosity, we said. At worst, an offensive abomination. Others found it *hot*. There was a movie made from
this book, then a few more, but they have since passed from collective
consciousness. So, too, the younger body of the arrogant man who
once mocked the phenomenon. Like the book, its one-time heated
relevance, its power to arouse, if not obsession then at least basic curiosity, had significantly (and predictably) diminished under its poorly
designed structure, its music-less, derivative form.

But now it has returned to me—the book, the body, the *heat*—on
this cold island, in the middle of a rare and intense uninterrupted

conversation between two handholding, snuggly, otherwise domestic, preoccupied fifty-something travelers. A newly extreme eroticism not articulated in this or any other tome I have encountered.

What, pray god, could be next for us in this tantalizing Arctic playroom?

There is a buzzing.

Her cell phone. She grunts displeasure and lifts the device to her face. A somehow familiar voice erupts from the plastic, a teenager from another world. He is complaining that, in his parents' absence, his grandmother is making him weed the front flower garden. He is now developing a pimply rash on his legs and arms, just in time for his big date at the pool. In a voice not unlike the screaming gulls, he claims this is a punishment he did not ask for and does not deserve.

Might she intervene?

"No!" she commands. "Do what Grandma says and don't call again, unless it's an emergency."

"*This IS an EMERG...*" She terminates the call.

I. Am. In. Awe.

There will be no more reaching her in this place. Or me. The cord has been cut—transformed into this conversational pleasure whip. This French Intellectual Tickler. This sensual, spiritual string connecting two slightly crumpled Dixie cups. She retakes my hand.

Intensity rising!

"Now, where were we, my man? Kant's categorical imperative?"

What is the safety word?!

"I don't know about you, but I've always found this concept to be ..."

THE WORD!

∎

When I awaken, we are hiking up a great green wave of earth that threatens to launch us into the clouds. My thighs are burning.

How did we choose such a difficult path?

Perhaps there was no choice. Grímsey, I recall, is the top of a mountain, its roots extending beneath ocean depths. It was thrust upward by geothermal and volcanic activity, a hot emulsion out of the Tjörnes rift zone, where the North American and Eurasian tectonic plates once collided and are now pulling apart, causing tremblings. The town of Dalvík, the very port we had departed this morning, contains no older structures, for they were all leveled by a devastating earthquake in 1934—two thousand people losing their homes, set to flight.

It occurs to me how difficult it is for anything to stay together.

As we ascend this heretofore unknown (to us) mountain, we are no longer holding hands, no longer wielding the conversational pleasure whip, due to the heavy breathing, groping for oxygen. The medulla oblongata is working overtime. But we are rewarded at the top with the grandest of views. To the south, a series of magnificent cliffs, each a massive promontory slicing into the sea, wedge-like, as if the bows of Viking long ships. Before them, the great expanse of ice-fed seas.

Adventure.

Death.

I am still hungry.

We sit down on the grass and bring forth delicacies from our backpacks: peanut butter sandwiches, crackers, cheese, cookies. We eat the cookies first, out of unconscious habit, for in a parallel world they are the first to be depleted by younglings, leaving nothing to satisfy more mature cravings. With our thumbs, we wipe the smudges of chocolate from each other's lips. This makes us laugh. I recall chess games. We share random exclamations over the magnificent view, the disbelief that we are here. We congratulate ourselves for abandoning the predictable. Cutting the cord.

Finding the new place of liberation.

And it is then, without warning, we enter an elemental silence as rare and delicious as anything we have experienced that day or in decades. Not the complete absence of sound, for there is the roar of the ocean, the wind. Rather, a luxurious, inward space opening to un-mitigated presence. Uninterrupted awareness.

This moment, alone together, feels older than time.

I peer down at the great cliffs to the southeast. Birds circle in the air—gulls, tamaracks—above the sea mist and shattering waves. Then I see them: *puffins!* Not as many as on the riled-up cliffs of Básavík, but still numerous. In the foreground, there is a small group beneath the grassy ledge of the cliff. Some are perched on narrow promontories; others nestled into openings in the rock. Nests? Though they perch in close proximity, there are no noisy disputes or billings. They seem to have entered their own version of this elemental silence. They do not seem concerned about us. No curious, clownish onlookers. Instead, the hooded eyes of the puffins appear fixed on the ocean's surface, the immeasurable distance.

As if waiting.

For their mate, I imagine. Could it be said that the puffins, like others I know on this planet, have signed a kind of contract establish-ing dominant and submissive? Not between themselves as individuals, but inside. Between individuals and the dominant thing inside them.

The thing that now turns puffin eyes out to sea, and my own to the person beside me.

Earlier, she and I posed in structured ritual above a threshold that had already moved beyond us, beneath signs that marked distances more easily measured. But when it comes to this thing inside and be-tween two beings, even greater distances must be traversed—as vast and full of dangers as any that exist in the known universe. And over the years they must be crossed not once, but many times. Out at sea, alone, in the winter, you may one day return home to find the bound-aries that matter, inside and between, have shifted. The *Orbis* must be rolled to accommodate or be abandoned—the choice is yours. The effort can test the limits of what you think is endurable.

But then there are moments like this, when those boundaries have once again become magnetized, orienting, irresistibly beckoning you to cross over.

Who is this I have waited for?

Who is this that returns to me from winter seas?

■

When I awaken, we are descending.

I am wary. Isn't the descent when most people die on Everest or any major climb? The stage when, after the high view, the oxygen runs out, the body breaks, and the mind confronts its true place in the universe?

It doesn't take long.

Not far down the southern trail, edging the cliffs, we encounter a pair of sheep. Their wool is long, thick, and curly, and they have horns. When we stop to measure their mood, I notice a stray piece of rope near my feet. I release my love's hand to pick it up—the first mistake. She keeps walking, reverses briefly to remind me that we should return to the harbor soon. I tell her no worries, I'll catch up. I want to take some pictures.

This is a lie: I have a rope to consider.

It is bright yellow, less than a foot in length, having clearly been severed at either end with a sharp instrument. It isn't particularly thick, maybe half an inch, but retains some rigidity. When I pull on either end, its strength is revealed.

A person might use it to climb.

Or to bind.

The proximity to the cliff suggests climbing, and I recall again that people have rappelled down such cliffs all over Grímsey, to retrieve eggs. But these cliffs are special, the very ones we admired from our picnic on high, inside that sweet moment of unmitigated presence. In my mind, I extend the rope to the edge of the precipice and over. Somewhere beneath, in the cliff side, are the puffins we observed while eating cookies. I cannot see them now, but I can somehow feel their watchfulness, their silence, and I am drawn into it—we are, in this moment, experiencing the same view, peering across the same expanse of ocean, sky, future.

I am no longer the creature merely watching other creatures watch and wait.

For what?

I had thought a mate, but the ground here isn't purring from lustful anticipation. The view feels less magnificent, more terrifying—exposure to the elements, proximity to a sheer drop-off.

The pufflings will make that same descent in the darkening autumn, when they fledge. Their wings will still be small and weak; many will be lost. Survivors will follow the moon out to sea, like baby sea turtles, returning in a few years to become flickering candles on the billing grounds. Or not. They can get confused on that initial flight by false luminosities—ship beacons and streetlights. False borders. Instead of landing on moonlit waves, they land on the decks of stalwart fishing vessels and on village cobblestones.

On the Icelandic island of Heimaey, where in 1913 a hot fissure spewed lava, there is an annual tradition of children rescuing pufflings who, disillusioned, skid onto their sidewalks and yards. The little birds are fed, weighed, measured, and tagged before being released.

One puffling rescuing another.

This IS an EMERG…

But right now my eyes are not those of the puffling, nor of the expectant young lover, but of those who watch across the void for the ones they have made. The little ones we have been given to feed, to dote on, and then give over to the world, hopefully returning, saved by their own skill or by the unseen charity of strangers or by chance. Each representing one singular moment of being lost in another, one year or many years of existence, yet each an extension of all the years that have been or ever will be for you and your kind.

The cord that can never be cut.

Yet here in my hand, is the severed rope. Below me are the cliffs where, in decades past, starving men descended. People so hungry they

ate the grass. As well as these birds and their eggs—the only ones—
heated over burning chessboards.

How to feed the children?

I want to believe starvation times on Grímsey are over, that the
choice, the contract that was once made can now, through new laws
and science and human decency, be unmade. On a planet that should
have plenty for all. Plenty of food and science and decency.

But then I arrive at this unwelcome cove of memory: a few years
ago there was a puffin nest on coastal Maine, among a centuries-old
colony restored to about a thousand birds, after near extinction from
hunting. From ropes and nets. There was an egg in that nest and above
it was a camera—the Puffin Cam, broadcasting to thousands of school
children across the globe.

Here is what the children saw.

The one egg a year, muddy white, is in the nest. The parents are
taking turns warming it, as is their way, nestling the egg in a featherless
flap of flesh on their undersides. The warmest, most vulnerable place
on their bodies. A little puffball emerges from the shell—someone
somewhere names it "Petey." Petey is hungry. The parents take flight,
seeking hake or herring or silvery sandeels. The fish hang from their
clown beaks, soft and thin, like the cellophane noodles once consumed
by a young couple on winter evenings before playing chess.

This is love.

But then one day the herring and the hake and sand eels cannot
be found.

The parents, with stubby wings better suited for swimming, must
fly farther and farther north, where these fish have retreated. Because
a place this cold shouldn't be so *hot*. Many don't return. They wash
up on distant shores, emaciated. Others become too exhausted and
no longer try. These exhausted, hungry parents find butterfish instead,
readily available. They sort of look like the other fish, only coin-shaped
and bigger than they usually are (again, the heat).

Back on the Puffin Cam, Petey is fed a butterfish by his parents. He holds it in his beak, tips his head back, tries to swallow, but the fish is too large. He tries again, chokes, then gives up. Petey is trembling. His parents bring him more butterfish, but it is the same: the choking, the trembling. Petey becomes sleepier and sleepier. One day, he doesn't wake up.

In front of all those eyes, watching.

Like all these eyes, on this cliff and others, in the Westons—where Gordon Ramsey swung his butterfly net—where last year nearly all the pufflings starved and there hasn't been a new, full generation created in more than a decade. All those eyes, on the edge of oblivion, watching. Including mine, right now. Wondering what waits for us and our own, on the deep horizon. Which ropes already bind and ensnare us? Which shall we yet be forced to descend?

Stop, please!

We have to feed them! Why are they dying?

Enough!

The children are not returning!

What is THE WORD?

■

When I awaken, I am hurrying down the trail. My love has become a dot on the horizon. I come to where another trail veers west—is this the turn toward safe harbor? To Earl Grey and pastries?

Time is short.

I call to her, wave my arms: *come back to me!* When she arrives she is no longer green, but red with exertion and worry. The air has become uncomfortably *hot.*

Where are we? Which is the fastest way back?

The captain was very stern, she reminds me. Very *commanding.* If we are not there on time, we will have to wait for the next boat in two days. I ask her for the map. She asks me for the map. Neither of us has the map! More words are exchanged, decidedly unsweetened. A cacophony. I don't want to hear it—my eyes are still inside a puffin skull, staring at dead Petey and a rope. I commit to the thin, overland trail. She lags for a bit, deciding, then follows. I keep walking, way ahead of her now, over the rise. Out of sight.

Which is why I am the first to be attacked.

There is a rush of air and a sharp blow to the back of my head.

Kría!

I look up and see the scimitar wings, slicing, hovering above me.

Kría! Kría!

I look around and see them—the terns, the nests—and understand. They have traveled to Antarctica, to the moon and back, to do what they are doing here. To find their lifelong mate, to make the egg and raise the young, which they do only once every year or three. By the time they perish, they will have seen more of the globe than almost anything alive, surviving countless threats—familiar predators, unfamiliar weather. Storms. Poison. Starvation.

They know things.

Now here I come, stomping around in hiking boots, smelling of boat diesel and ignorance—*we were warned!* No use now. I am as naked and exposed as the giant egg-sucking rat I truly am. The offensive abomination. *The heat!*

Kría! Kría! Kría!

The tern army is launching itself into the sky, one by one. I hear a woman scream behind me. I start to run.

Thwap—another blow! *Motherfucker, that hurt!* Am I bleeding? I want to scream: *stop, please!* I want to negotiate terms! I won't hurt you! I am just like you and the puffins, a compassionate earthling in love, waiting, eyes on the same uncertain horizon, the shared apocalypse.

I care about the children!

Thwap! The tern hits me so hard this time it actually penetrates the cranium and enters my brain, past the medulla oblongata, right into the frontal Broca's area. It finds the words.

Kría! You are NOT one of us!

Kría! You ARE the apocalypse!

Kría! You have BROKEN the contract with the true and only DOMINANT!

Kría! You are the KILLER of younglings and LOVE!

Kría! There is no WORD that will save you from this PAIN!

Kría! This IS an EMER...!

I hear more human screams from somewhere behind me, but I cannot stop. Billing time is over. Empathy has outlived its status as something to be rewarded, for its own sake. And we will not receive it. All creatures see us, naked, through their own eyes. We have demanded too much of them. They and this *Jǫrð* will soon have nothing left to give us, except the final discipline. As contracted.

Thwap!

I am running now, desperate to escape. There is something rough in my hand—the rope! I stop and turn into the white noise of reckoning and heave it. It nearly nails one of the terns, and there is a moment's retreat, a small clearing in the swarm above my Seventh Chakra.

Kría! Kría!

I am gone.

∎

When I awaken, I am on the deck of the *Saefari*, at sea. The sun is shining, the waves calm, and I am sweating inside a pointless rain jacket. Someone is beside me, disheveled and silent. A woman I think. Do I know her? I taste something sweet and bitter in my mouth. Must have reached Sandvík in time to get a blueberry muffin and a cup of Earl Grey.

What was the rush again?

My head hurts.

A man's voice interrupts: *hey, you!*

A sailor with an accent. On the other side of the deck, a middle-aged blonde head turns in recognition.

I have what you want!

The sailor approaches with a cardboard carton. He opens it before her eyes, like a jewelry case. Four muddied white eggs.

Oh, yes! she exclaims in American, clapping. *Yes! Yes!*

She draws in close, touches his shoulder, kisses his cheek. His neck goes crimson.

Thank you!

There is a loud, collective *awwww*, but it is not for them. Eyes are elsewhere.

A whale has just emerged from the deep. Its scarred back is blue-grey and massive, its essence bigger than anything we can know. The blonde American woman turns away from her sailor to peer overboard. The eggs are forgotten.

The giant moves alongside us for a minute or so, gently parting the waters, a parallel world. People are enthralled, they cry out. They cry. *So beautiful!* Then it disappears before our eyes, into the depths.

She slips her arm in mine.

We are alone together. *This is love.*

It is hot.

There are no words.

MY PREGAME PEP TALKS

The Impossible Season

GAME 1: *At Sioux City North, August 24, 2018*

OK, guys, listen up. I know some of you may be wondering why I am speaking to you here in the locker room before the big football game—the start of what I know is going to be a triumphant season! The short answer is that Coach invited me, and I want to thank him right off the bat for thinking outside the box. That's what all the great ones do.

Let's face it, last season didn't go so well, and Coach is looking for new ways to put this program back on the expressway to winning. I guess he heard somewhere that I am an inspirational nature writer and teacher, and thought I could share a few encouraging words to give you that extra edge before going out there to lay it all on the line for Council Bluffs Abraham Lincoln High School. Something beyond the Xs and Os. I'm not exactly sure where he got his information, but when he called, I answered.

Number one, as most of you know, I am the father of your starting middle linebacker and senior captain, Ben Price, who is kind of hiding over there behind Blutowski—*Hi there, buddy!* So I have a personal reason for wanting you to succeed this season. I'm also here for your parents, most of whom have spent your football games—and countless practices, scrimmages, and camps—relegated to watching from the sidelines or stands, entirely helpless, wishing they could suit up and make a difference. If they have the time, that is, since a number of them are single parenting, working multiple jobs and night shifts.

You'll be thankful to know I won't be suiting up, but I am still here to try to make a difference—for you, your parents, our school, our community. Our world!

And thanks to Coach, I'll be doing it all season!

I want to start off by promising I will always be real with you guys. I won't try to sell you a wheelbarrow full of BS. The hard truth is that over the last two seasons, AL has won a total of five games. This year, Lynx football is ranked near the bottom of the entire state in 4A. This could be one of the reasons that, despite being a relatively large school of 1,300 students, you have a total of eight seniors on the team, one of them a foreign exchange student from Sweden. Hardly anyone believes in you.

I'm not saying that to get you down. I want you to use it as motivation!

So let's get right to it: tonight's opponent is one of the two teams you beat last year. That should give you hope. Also, their team name is the North Stars, and here's a tip from a literary pro: use their symbolism against them. The North Star, otherwise known as Polaris, is the only star in the sky that never moves, that never runs away when the going gets tough. It has guided lost men home and directed ships to places that at first seemed impossible to reach—like you guys and the Iowa high school football playoffs! Prior to the Civil War, Polaris guided escaped slaves north to freedom, along the secret underground railroad. They sang about it in spirituals like "Follow the Drinking Gourd," which was actually simple code because the way you locate the North Star is by following the edge of the Big Dipper straight up. So that constellation was at once a symbol of the thirst for freedom, and a navigation tool on the journey north.

Did you know that Council Bluffs was one of the stops on the underground railroad? That's part of the history of the community you play for, and you should be proud of it, even if it was almost two centuries ago.

But like I said, I'll always be real with you boys, and here it is: Polaris wasn't always the North Star. Around 12,000 BCE that honor belonged to the star Vega, and in the year 13,727, thanks to the slow wobble of the Earth's axis, it will once again be Vega. But your opponent doesn't need to know that.

Or do they?

Maybe that's a little something to add to your trash talking repertoire—"Hey guys, you might be North Stars now, but not in another 12,000 years!" Get inside their heads a little.

Anyway, the point is that the North Star is out there tonight, both real and symbolic, to guide you to the end zone, to lead you to freedom from whatever it is that's keeping you from realizing your potential, in your life as well as on the field. Just look up to find that Big Dipper, so that all that inner thirstiness, whatever it is you are thirsty for, might be quenched.

And that's what I want to ask you boys right now: Are you thirsty? *Are you?!*

Now bring it in! On three ... *for the Dipper!*

Final Score: North Stars 47 – Lynx 20.

GAME 2: *At Denison-Schleswig, August 31, 2018*

OK, guys, let's be honest: last week wasn't how we'd hoped to start the season. As Coach said in the paper, and I quote: "I thought there was a lack of execution and we've got to find a way to improve that." Insights like that are exactly why he's the admiral of this battleship.

I know Coach had you examine a lot of film over the last week, which is good, but you can't let the past weigh you down. Not just the last game, but last season and the season before that. That's yesterday's news and as Coach Ferentz of the Iowa Hawkeyes always says after a disappointing game or season, you just have to "flush it." And he should know.

So let's talk about "execution," but from a slightly different angle.

When you go out there tonight, you'll notice the distinct smell of animal feces in the air—there's no flushing that stench away, I promise you. It's from the nearby meatpacking plant, where it could be said hundreds of thousands of cows and pigs are "executed" every year. A little wordplay there, but in all seriousness, the burgers most of us ate this week came from this stink-factory or one very much like it. That includes yours truly—I may be a nature writer, but I'm not above digging into a double cheeseburger with fries every now and then. And don't even get me started on bacon! I'm definitely not above the ethical muck.

Truth is, however, a lot of people who live in this town depend on the jobs at that processing plant. Among them are many Latino immigrants and their families. A little civics lesson: every presidential election cycle, people will inevitably say that Iowa shouldn't be the first-in-the-nation caucus because it isn't diverse enough. And when you study the stats overall, that appears to be the case—only around fifteen percent is of a minority population in this state. Even lower when it comes to this football team, though thanks to your Swedish kicker, you might technically be called "international."

Frankly, boys, I agree, and I'm sure you do too, that our current electoral system disenfranchises many urban and minority voters. It should be abolished. But here's the point: in Denison, a town of 8,400, half the population is Latino—some long-time residents, some newly arrived. There are many Latino-owned businesses, which have helped restore this small town, economically and culturally. Across Iowa, the Latino population has grown 480 percent between 1990 and this year, and that number is expected to double in the next few decades. In fact, this very county, Crawford, is on track to be the first Latino majority county in Iowa.

That's another reason for a place to be proud.

Especially in a congressional district represented by hometown boy, Steve King, who has publicly questioned why "white supremacist" has become such a negative term. He also said about Mexican immigrants: "For everyone who's a valedictorian, there's another hundred out there who weigh 130 pounds—and they've got calves the size of cantaloupes because they're hauling seventy-five pounds of marijuana across the desert."

I hate to give Team White Supremacist any more airtime, but their Coach Steve King reminds us of something important: when your bus rolled into Denison, it was also arriving at an unfortunate source of who we are in relationship to this world. *Fear.* That, too, is what you are smelling in the air, and it stinks.

Maybe that fear includes your opponent—you *know* they are crapping their pants right now thinking about your daunting defense. Then again, maybe a few of those players are also afraid they'll come home from tonight's game to discover some of their family members have been arrested and threatened with deportation. Or just threatened. Maybe they are themselves afraid of deportation, since the current administration has sought to eliminate the DREAM Act. Or maybe they're afraid for those at the southern border, children even, who are wrapped in foil and living in cages near fences that Coach Steve King proposed electrifying. Maybe someone they know has died in the desert or in an overpacked boxcar, trying to make it right here to Denison, Iowa—which actually happened in 2002—to enjoy a life where Friday night is about stadium lights and not search lights. Where losing a football game is the worst that can happen, rather than losing your life in the darkness of the Sonora.

On a slightly different note, when I first heard Denison's team name was the Monarchs, I confess I thought they were referring to the butterflies.

Did you know that the monarchs you are seeing now will soon

migrate three thousand miles to winter in the highlands of Central Mexico? They recognize no borders. In early November, around El Día de los Muertos, they will arrive at the same mountain forest of oyamel fir trees that they have been returning to for centuries. The local people in Michoacán believe the butterflies to be the souls of dead children, returning home.

But maybe it could be said that Iowa is their home, too, since they worked so hard and sacrificed so much to reach it. Coach always says you need to *earn* it, and haven't they? Regardless, I can't imagine this place without such courage and beauty.

Can you?

So let's just think about that as we bring it in! On three ... *for the butterflies! For the children!*

Final Score: Monarchs 42 – Lynx 6.

GAME 3: *Lewis Central High School (Council Bluffs), September 7, 2018*

Truth, boys, I'm feeling a little uncertain about my speech last week. I worry it might have been too intimidating—I know it's difficult to live up to the physical and spiritual endurance of the monarch butterfly or people who have risked death to reach safety and freedom. No one expects that of you! Nor, unfortunately, do we expect it of the politicians who write environmental and immigration policies, but that's another issue.

The more immediate concern is the subsequent exodus of so many players from the team. Ben tells me that half of the offensive line quit to join the cheer squad, which at first I didn't believe, but it has since been confirmed. Not to put down the cheer squad, but I'm sure that was a tough pill to swallow.

Even tougher, the fact that your starting running back quit the team and has joined tonight's opponent, the LC Titans, your most hated cross-town rival. To their credit, the LC coaches—one of whom, as you know, used to be the head coach here at AL—is forcing him to sit out this game. But I hear that hasn't stopped this former teammate from right now sitting in your student section, wearing an LC Titans t-shirt. I also heard that one of your teammates, who may or may not be related to me, called him a "fat cow" to his face during pregame warm-ups.

I don't condone name-calling, but I admire the spunk.

Coach said in the paper that leading up to this first home game against a highly ranked opponent, "We don't talk about them; we talk about us. We need to get our team better." Those are wise and lyrical words, and I agree with him that we need to do some talking about us. That's pretty much what a nonfiction writer like me does for a living. In fact, during a graduate school writing workshop—you think football is brutal!—someone quipped that everything I write should be subtitled, "Anyway, back to me!" Maybe that needs to be our new team slogan: "Anyway, back to us!"

So who is "us"? What do we stand for as a team?

Here again, language can be helpful.

Similes, for instance, which compare one thing to another, different thing—and heads-up, you might want to jot this down for your next standardized test. Among their many uses, similes can be very helpful for midwesterners like us who prefer not to speak in direct ways about our inner pain. So instead of saying, "We are demoralized by losing all these football games and seeing our teammates quit on us"; we would instead say, "We feel *like* the critically endangered Salt Creek tiger beetles of central Nebraska." Or instead of saying, "Lewis Central has a bigger and better football team because they're from the suburbs, including the Bent Tree Golf Course subdivision, and have more money and extracurricular programs than we do and so parents transfer their kids there and head coaches quit here to become assistant coaches there," we can say, "That school district is *like* a fat cow."

You see, similes can be kind of fun, once you get going. Now let's hear a few from you!

OK, I guess you guys are feeling a little shy tonight, probably nerves before the big game. That's totally understandable, so let me offer some positive similes to get you pumped up. "We are Abraham Lincoln High School, and we are *like* a lynx, crafty with broad paw pads that can walk on top of snow and all adversity!" Or "We are *like* a cumulonimbus cloud that when seen from below looks flat and ugly, but which can sometimes reach seventy thousand feet high and weigh as much as a mountain and is capable of flattening entire towns!" Or "We are *like* dust motes, small and invisible and easily brushed aside— until we drift into a game-day sunbeam and become sparkly *like* magic pixie dust!" And we could all use a little of that magic pixie dust right now, couldn't we boys?

Yes, Peter, we want to fly!!!

Anyway, those are just suggestions—I'm sure you can come up with a few on your own, maybe better ones. Like all good teachers, I'm just the guide on the side, not the sage on the stage. It's not about me or you, it's about "us." *Anyway, back to us!* Think about that as you get out there and beat these guys. There's a good crowd tonight, and thanks to your former linemen, the cheer squad should be especially loud. Feed off their energy!

Now bring it in! On three ... *for the Pixies!*

Final Score: Titans 59 – Lynx 7

GAME 4: *Sioux City East High School, September 14, 2018*

Let's face it, last week's game was *like* being hit by a freight train. That's another simile, but it is also what the literary pros might call a *cliché*, though if they were here in this locker room, I'd tell them straight up that sometimes clichés speak the truth. That's how they become clichés!

Case in point, a lot of guys got hurt last week, including both starting quarterbacks, which literally happens when you are hit by a freight train. Or, if you want to mix it up a little, maybe change "freight train" to something less expected, more ecocentric, such as "charging bison bull."

Either way, it was awful to watch. Truly terrifying. Ben's mom and I were sitting near the parents of one of the quarterbacks, and the looks on their faces when their son limped off the field was, well, terrifying. We recalled that it could be any one of our boys suffering that injury or something far worse.

Not that we could ever forget. It's a risk that comes with playing football, as you know, and it has given some of us parents more than a few sleepless nights. It's not just about being "paranoid," as Ben sometimes puts it. In recent years, a lot of new information has come out about CTE, which is short for chronic traumatic encephalopathy. It's caused by multiple concussions to the brain, which can occur in football and, over time, lead to memory loss, impaired judgment, and eventual dementia.

No doubt the growing science on CTE is among the reasons participation in high school football is down across the country. Maybe even here, since the low roster numbers ensure that each player will be on the field a lot more minutes than usual, on both sides of the ball, against opponents that are far larger, far more refreshed, and far better equipped. So it could be the lack of teammates is not entirely about your losing record.

Now, there are flex helmets available, which are safer, but as you know, our team only has around a dozen. Yes, Ben has one of them, but it's not because his father is a famous nature writer and pulled strings. It's because they only give them to the senior starters—which, on the bright side, means there should be more than a few left over. I'm not sure why we don't have more of them. They're expensive, and maybe after the district remodeled the old stadium and gave the superintendent a raise, they didn't have any cash left over to protect your brains.

Anyway, it's a tough call as a parent.

I can tell you that Ben's mom and I considered stopping him from playing tackle football each year since he started. We've received a lot of criticism about that and I'll be true: much of it is justified. All I can say is each situation is different, and here's how it went with us and Ben. Believe it or not, your stud of a captain once struggled with health issues—and I don't think I'm embarrassing him by saying that. He talks about it openly, as a matter of pride. He turned his situation around with lots of determination and sweat. But what he may not recall is that his pediatrician told us when he was in elementary school that he was at a high risk for developing diabetes. He was pretty overweight and there was family history. His blood tests were scary.

I know some of you don't think diabetes is all that serious—Ben showed me a popular YouTube video that turns a public awareness message on diabetes by actor Wilford Brimley into some kind of weird rap song. It's supposed to be funny, but I can assure you this disease is nothing to laugh at, especially in young people. And it's expensive, way more than flex helmets. That's why the doctor strongly urged us to get him to exercise and eat right. *Immediately.* We were already preparing healthy meals, but we couldn't entirely control what he ate when he was hanging out with friends, which was a lot, because he's a popular guy. Unlike me at his age. Or even now.

But the biggest struggle was the exercise. Ben didn't like it and mostly refused to do it. There was a lot of crying and frustration, on both sides, and some evidence in him of growing depression, which also runs in the family.

In short, we were worried out of our minds.

Then Ben discovered football. I don't know how it happened exactly, because I never played the game and frankly had some issues with the über-machoism it seemed to promote. For Ben, though, it was about friendships and finding an outlet for all this pent-up energy he had inside, a particular kind of outlet that spoke to the particular kind of energy inside his particular kind of body. Those particulars are a big reason why anyone gravitates toward one sport over another, aren't they?

The particulars of his younger brother Spencer's lanky body, in contrast, require that he never, ever be allowed near a football field. Plus, he doesn't have great hand-eye coordination, so he doesn't like having a ball thrown at his face. Then again, he could probably play wide receiver for this team, since more often than not the quarterback is tackled before he can complete a pass.

Sorry, just a little humor there, to keep you loose.

As I was saying, football clicked with Ben. Suddenly, we couldn't stop him from exercising—running sprints with his teammates in the dog days of July, named for the summer constellation of Canis Major, or working out at the gym with those same guys in February, known by the Lakota as *Cannapopa Wi*, "Moon When the Trees Crack from the Cold." All year long. He not only lost excess weight and gained muscle, but according to his pediatrician, the risk of diabetes is now dramatically reduced. His spirit soared sky-high! Yes, he tried other sports, including swimming and track, which ironically is the only time he got a concussion, when a teammate accidentally hit him in the head with a discus.

For Ben, though, it's always been about football. And despite everything we know about the risks, when we consider where this boy we love might have ended up without this sport, we can't help but feel some gratitude.

Mixed in with the guilt and the terror.

But a word to the wise: while you're out there, try not to think about how terrified and guilty your parents feel. Even if it is easier to spot their faces in the stands, thanks to the dwindling crowds. Don't fret about any of that. Just get out there and play, because that's how it all started for you guys, right? As play.

Now bring it in! On three ... *for Wilford Brimley!*

Final Score: Warriors 49 – Lynx 0

GAME 6: *Ames High School, Homecoming, September 28, 2018*

Sorry about missing last week's game at Urbandale, guys. I thought maybe my locker room talks weren't helping much, since the last one was followed by the biggest loss by Abraham Lincoln since perhaps the Civil War. Seriously, though, I thought you could use the extra time with Coach during pregame, going over the Xs and Os. The J-Hawks beat you 49–6, so I guess it didn't make much of a difference, which in a way is a relief.

OK, maybe that didn't come out right.

Here's the point: I'm back in the huddle and won't ever let you down again. That's another cliché, maybe two, but as I said, there's truth in it. Unlike some of your former teammates, and most of the fan base, I'm here for the long haul and rededicated to helping you and Coach turn this season around.

I'm not quitting on you guys!

That starts with even more self-reflection as a team, really digging deep inside the cerebral walnut, to get at the meat. And big surprise to anyone who's read my work, I'm going to begin with me. Like some of you, I set up a one-on-one meeting with Coach to ask him how to improve my game-day performance. After a long pause, during which I could tell Coach was doing a lot of thinking—he's a thinker, this guy— he informed me that my talks can go on a little long and sometimes get off track. I respect that. I've heard it before. That's the same thing my colleagues at work say about my emails. But what can I do? *I'm a writer!*

Correction, here's what I can do: *my best.*

That's all Coach or any of you ask of each other, right? Sometimes, though, we can be afraid to give it our all, because we are afraid of failure. I know at Denison I talked about how fear is at the center of existence, but one thing we shouldn't be afraid of is failure—trust me, it's something you can get used to. Nor should we be afraid to admit our mistakes and keep trying to improve. I learned that from some of the greats.

For instance, one of my heroes off the gridiron is a certain six-teenth-century French nobleman and writer by the name of Michel de Montaigne. Known to his buddies as "Big Monty," he grew up pretty wealthy—he would have probably attended some high school like Des Moines Dowling, because he was rich and also Catholic. Or at least his father was, while his mother was a Protestant convert with Sephardic Jewish ancestry, which was a bit of a problem back then because there were a lot of religious wars going on all over Europe. In Spain, where his mother's family came from, the Inquisition was still happening. I'm sure some of you have studied the Inquisition in class or, if you're LGBTQ in this country, are actually living it.

Sorry, Coach. *Stay on track!*

Big Monty eventually got fed up with life in the fast lane and re-treated to his ancestral estate to get his head on straight. He was wor-ried about a lot of things: religious wars, plague, body odor, and how people didn't read enough books because they were all in Latin, to name just a few.

But he didn't give up!

Just like Bradbury Robinson who, in 1905, invented the forward pass in football, Michel de Montaigne decided to change the game forever. He invented this little thing you might have heard of, called … *The Essay.* It actually comes from the French word *essayer*, which means to "try" or "attempt" or "do your best." Big Monty believed that if you use the essay to openly explore and write about your own mistakes or half-baked "attempts" (like, for instance, the game against Sioux City East), learning from them and even forgiving them, you might become a wiser, happier human being. You might also extend that understand-ing and forgiveness to your so-called enemies. As Big Monty put it, "Each man bears the entire form of man's estate."

In gender-neutral terms, that means you should treat every individ-ual as belonging to the same flawed, but sacred human family. In the process, you might make the world a better place.

In that spirit, I'd like to offer up a personal failure that happened just a few minutes ago. I bumped into one of Ben's old coaches in the stands, from his years in the peewee football league, who moved out of town several years ago. He has a couple of sons, one of whom helped his dad coach when he was in high school. I'll call this son, Doogie. I asked how Doogie was doing, and the coach said great, and that he was actually throwing a gender reveal party this weekend. That's why the whole family was back in town. I told him I had actually never heard of such a party, but thought it was wonderful the family was so supportive of their loved one coming out as their true gender, whether bi, pan, genderqueer, agender, or any gender on the beautiful spectrum of human identity. We need more of that sort of love and support in America, I said.

That's when Ben's mom elbowed me in the ribs and told me what a gender reveal party really is.

Everyone laughed, including the coach, but for me it was still embarrassing. Humiliating, even—a word you're not unfamiliar with this season. I mean, shouldn't I have known this already? I had to forgive myself. But here's the thing: I learned something. I won't make that mistake again, even though in all honesty I believe there should be that other kind of gender reveal party. Maybe it would help end the Inquisition.

At this point, I was planning to invite you to do some out-loud self-reflection of your own, but Coach is signaling to wrap things up. Consider it homework. Now go out there and really *essayer* to beat this team!

Bring it in! On three … *for Michel de Montaigne!*

Final Score: Little Cyclones 49 – Lynx 3

GAME 7: *West Des Moines Valley High School, October 5, 2018*

I want to thank you guys for taking my words to heart last week. I could tell you really tried, really *attempted* to win, even though the final score doesn't reflect it. Big Monty would have been proud!

Seriously, you fought hard and were only down a point at half-time. Even Coach said in the paper, and I quote: "That was probably the brightest moment—that first quarter and a half—that we've had all year, so we need to build on that." Amazing. Razor-sharp analysis like that is why this guy gets paid the big bucks.

OK, that last bit is what the literary pros might call *sarcasm*, and I should probably apologize for it. If you can't tell, I'm a little on edge tonight. Valley isn't just any old game for me.

This time, it's personal.

The reason, you ask? Let me tell you a little story about a guy I knew who was a freshman at the University of Iowa in the 1980s, but who was the same age as some of you seniors, because his parents enrolled him a bit too early in kindergarten. I guess his mother thought this four-year-old's intelligence was "off the charts," as they say nowadays, so no judgment. The consequence, however, was that he spent most of his youth way behind his peers physically. He loved sports, and had some natural athletic talent, but he was too small to play basketball or football. Believe me, he tried.

So he took up wrestling while still in elementary school and was pretty good. He won a lot. When he moved to junior high, he was excited to go out for the team, and was still pretty good, but he was also ruthlessly bullied by some of his so-called teammates. To give you a sense of what he was up against, his old wrestling partner is now serving life in prison for kidnapping his wife and six-year-old daughter at gunpoint and threatening to kill them. Then he burned down their house.

Long story short, this kid I'm talking about quit wrestling and became a tennis player. There was no bullying on the tennis team, even though the sport is often called "gentlemen's boxing." His teammates seemed to understand him, maybe because they had also been bullied. They even gave him a cool nickname, "the Broaster," because he had a wicked forehand. Legendary, really. There wasn't much pressure to win in tennis because almost no one was watching. But this kid did win and even if no one remembers that his school had a boy's tennis team back then, this guy can replay every detail of every victory in his mind. It kind of saved him.

But that doesn't mean he forgot the bullying. People pretend like the damage done by those little monsters ends at the doors of high school. Everyone just moves on after graduation. Just flushes it. That's not the case for all.

For instance, this kid I'm talking about had a friend at that same junior high, who I'll call Mark. They sometimes walked home together after school. Mark's family didn't have a lot of money, so no fancy Izod crew shirts or tortoise-shell glasses for him. No, Mark wore plain white t-shirts and black horn-rimmed glasses, because that's the only style of eyewear his dad's factory bosses offered to purchase for their employees and their families. Mark was bullied relentlessly about the glasses and everything else—way more than this other kid I'm talking about. And he didn't belong to any sports teams or extracurriculars that might have saved him, because he had to work after school.

There was this one guy who was especially cruel to Mark. I'll call him Dick. He was fairly popular at the school, in the way cruel people often are, and he had the meanest eyes you can imagine. Shark's eyes. *Doll's* eyes. I'll spare you the details of what Dick did to Mark, but it was bad. The teachers did nothing about it. Maybe they didn't see it. But this other kid I'm talking about saw it, which is why they sometimes walked home from school together, for protection.

After graduation, he and Mark fell out of touch, but he learned years later that Mark had since tried to kill himself, and more than once. He'd been hospitalized. When this guy I'm talking about went to one of his high school reunions, he had hoped against the odds that Mark might be there. He wasn't. Instead, the bully who had tormented him was there. Dick had clearly moved on, had a family, a decent job. Respected in his community. He'd flushed it. But his mean eyes hadn't changed. They were exactly the same. Even so, this guy I'm talking about really tried, really *essayé-d* to look at Dick the way Michel de Montaigne might, as part of the same human estate, but then Dick came up to him at the bar and tried to chit-chat, as if nothing had ever happened. This guy I'm talking about just waved a hand in front of Dick's face and went back to his table.

For those of you who don't know, that's midwestern for: *go fuck yourself, you fucking soul murderer!*

Sorry about the language, boys, but it was heartfelt. Anyway, unlike Mark, the kid I'm talking about escaped to college, where he grew a couple of inches and got a fresh start. For the most part, he just wanted to forget about high school, but then he encountered a guy from West Des Moines Valley High who lived on his dorm floor. I'll call him Hermie, because he kind of looked like that elf from the Rankin/Bass *Rudolph the Red-Nosed Reindeer* television special. And he wanted to be a dentist.

He was pretty stuck up, this guy from Valley, which isn't a crime in itself, but he took it to a whole other level. For instance, he designated himself "captain" of the intramural basketball team, and since there were too many players, he decided to divide us up into two teams according to where we resided on the dorm floor. Only, he gerrymandered the dividing line, so his team magically got all the tall guys who had started in high school. Sort of *like* a state legislature with congressional districts.

As you can probably guess, the guy I'm talking about wasn't selected for Hermie's Dream Team. Neither was his roommate, who I'll call Stan. Stan was older than most of the guys on the floor, and in the dorms in general, and unfortunately that year he had been assigned to a triple with this guy I'm talking about and a sophomore who was pretty nice, but who had a bit of a binge-drinking issue. He and Stan shared the bunk bed. Sometimes this other roommate would come home from a night of boozing, pass out in the top bunk, and pee right through the mattress onto Stan.

That didn't make Stan's year any easier. Neither did the fact that he had an involuntary physical tic. Every time Stan got especially excited or laughed or got peed on, he would clap his hands loudly and rub them together super-fast and bend over or sit up super fast and say something that sounded like *"Tschüss!"*—which, interestingly, is how Germans say, "So long, have a nice day!"

Anyway, Stan's condition didn't go unnoticed by this guy from Valley, who imitated it constantly.

Those on the leftover basketball team invited Stan to join, and let's just say they could tell he was pretty excited about it. Their team's name was Sticky Fingers, *which isn't what you're thinking, Blutowski*—it was actually named after the Rolling Stones album! But I guess that album was named after that other thing, so whatever. Sticky Fingers didn't have a starting lineup, and everyone got equal playing time. They actually ended up winning a bunch of games and having fun together. Lifetime friendships were forged.

But the game they had circled on the calendar, of course, was the cross-hall rivalry. When the big day arrived, Hermie walked onto the court with a giant boom box playing "Eminence Front" by The Who, because that was the name of their team. Following the opening tip-off, the teams exchanged leads in a spirited battle. The guy I'm talking about was having one of his best games, scoring in double figures. Then Hermie decided he'd try to shut him down and started pushing him around when the refs weren't looking and elbowing him in the ribs and jaw, sort of like those bullies did to him and Mark in junior high.

It must have triggered something, because early in the second half, Hermie pulled down a rebound, and this guy I'm talking about reached from behind, grabbed the ball, and pulled him down onto the court, hard, so he sort of slammed his head. Hermie freaked out and charged the guy, trying to put some kind of wrestling move on him, but that went nowhere—like I said, he had been a pretty good wrestler. The refs kicked Hermie out of the game (remember, it's always the one who *retaliates* that gets caught), and he watched from the bench as Sticky Fingers beat his carefully constructed eminent Dream Team.

But the highlight for all, besides the fight and the final score, was when Stan drove the length of the court with five seconds to go and, miraculously, tossed in a layup—his only score of the season! All the Sticky Fingers were on their feet cheering, jumping up and down in slow motion. It was a real-life Cinderella moment! A classic! Some think it should be a movie.

This may come as a surprise, but that guy I was talking about? That was me.

I know it's hard to imagine looking at the imposing man standing before you, the famous author with all the words and the wisdom. But here's the truth: no matter who we become as grown-ups, I'm not sure we ever leave those earlier selves behind. Who you are now, what you are feeling, how you and your friends, your loved ones, are treated will be remembered. How you treat others will be remembered. Try to be the one who is remembered with affection and respect.

But anyway, back to me: sitting somewhere on the other side of the stadium, grown-up Hermie might be watching his son on the field battling my son. I wish I could remember his last name, but I can't, so I want you to do me a favor and pretend that every one of those Valley players is *that guy*. I haven't ever asked this, but I want you to win this one for me, boys, and for Mark and Stan and every kid who's ever been overlooked or underestimated or bullied. Sort of like this entire team, this entire season.

The same estate, boys. The same estate!

So let's bring it in! On three … *for the Broaster!*

Final Score: Tigers 77 – Lynx 0

GAME 8: *At Des Moines North High School, October 12, 2018*

I admit it guys: last week's performance wasn't my best. To be honest, I feel like I kind of lost it a little. Maybe the pressure of this season is finally getting to me. Like Big Monty said, we're all human. I've apologized to Coach during another one-on-one and hope to win back his trust and yours. Also, Ben told me that the Valley players and coaches were actually pretty nice, so I guess I owe them an apology too. I'll try to do better tonight.

That's what a famous coach said about football, right? Just another name for "second chance!"

Speaking of famous coaches, yours put it beautifully in the paper last week, and I quote: "We still did some good things, and we have two games left to do more good things." Ponder that wisdom for the ages while you consider tonight's opponent, Des Moines North High School. The Polar Bears are currently ranked last in the state among Class 4A football teams. The Lynx are ranked second to last. So there's a lot at stake, though it isn't exactly reflected by the crowd size. In fact, it appears that we visiting fans may outnumber those for the home team. Maybe that has something to do with the fact that North hasn't won a game since 2016.

But don't get cocky—this team is just as thirsty as you are!

Knowing the challenge ahead, I really struggled this week to find the right words to give you guys the mental edge. Eventually, I decided to throw out the playbook and get back to basics, which I hear Coach has been doing at practices, as well. Basics like throwing, catching, running, and tackling.

For me, as a struggling wordsmith, it's about going back to Peter Elbow's basic freewriting technique. It begins with writing a subject or question at the top of the page and, for ten minutes, just dashing down whatever comes into your mind. Turn off that internal editor and just go! To others it looks like laziness, but actually you can come up with some pretty useful ideas when you set aside expectations.

So that's exactly what I did, and because "team" is just another word for "vulnerable," I brought the results of that exercise with me to this very locker room, where I'm going to share them with you, unedited, unprettified. *Raw.*

Just like in the NFL, I'm going to mic-up and take you inside my game.

My Peter Elbow Freewriting Subject: **POLAR BEARS**

Big, white, scary, with big sharp teeth that are dripping bloody seal chunks while running on ice flows. Ice flows, bright and cold. Too bright. Too white. Cracking and melting. More blue. Less white. Des Moines North High School. Global warming. Bad. UN report on global warming, just this week. Newspaper article—go get it! Got it! Team Earth up against it. Opponent: Human Greed and Stupidity. Gasoline and Bovine Flatulence. Denison. Pop-Tarts. Situation Dire. Hope? Article: "Earth's weather, health and ecosystems would be in better shape if the world's leaders could somehow limit future human-caused warming to 0.9 degrees Fahrenheit." Unlikely. "Draconian measures." Cheating. Unstoppable? New England Patriots. Read my lips! Only 0.9 degrees. List of benefits: 1) "Half as many people would suffer from lack of water"— Drought? Poisoned farm wells? Stay thirsty? 2) "There would be fewer deaths and illnesses from heat, smog and infectious diseases"—Ebola? Some other virus? Human stupidity as virus? 3) "Half as many animals with back bones and plants would lose the majority of their habitats"— Senators are safe. Polar Bears? Lynx? 4) "There would be substantially fewer heat waves, downpours and droughts"—Environmental disasters. Poverty. Vulnerable. Catastrophic Missouri River flooding? Catastrophic hail? Every year, it seems. Insurance? New siding? Which color? Sage green, maybe. Beige trim. Quote: Cornell climate scientist, "We have a monumental task in front of us, but it is not impossible. This is our chance to decide what the world will look like." Sounds like: "We still did some good things, and we have two games left to do more good things." Connection? 0.9 degrees. Of Kevin Bacon? Bacon. Yum.

That's step one of the Peter Elbow freewriting technique, and I know what some of you are thinking: *yikes*, this guy is really good, I could never do that! Remember, I'm a professional. Just dive in and let it flow—it's all good. All "off the charts!"

Now, after that initial brainstorm, take a deep breath and go back through what you've written to see if anything surprising pops out, some unexpected ideas, images, or juxtapositions. Something with a little heat to it. For example: "Less white. Des Moines North High School."

Whoa! Where did that come from? You want to find out.

You could do another freewriting session, but in this case, you feel a little hesitant, so you jump into some loosey-goosey internet research, just to see what turns up. You type in those keywords and, right away, you come across a website called *GreatSchools.org*. It claims to be "the leading national nonprofit empowering parents to unlock educational opportunities for their child. GreatSchools's trusted ratings and school information help parents find the right school for their family and improve schools in their communities."

You decide to look up Des Moines North High School, your opponent, and you see right off it has an overall *GreatSchools* ranking of one out of ten, and it's not the good kind of number one. You see that it gets the lowest possible ranking—"Very Concerning"—in categories such as College Readiness, Test Scores, Student Progress, Equity, and Chronically Absent.

But what really stands out is the truth you accidentally stumbled upon in your original freewriting session: North is "less white" than your high school. Way less. In fact, less white than any school in the conference. Students of color make up 75 percent of those attending that school. As opposed to, say, nearby suburban Ankeny Centennial High School, which is 90 percent white—you'll remember that Centennial beat you two years ago 62–13 and gave out free sympathy popcorn to visiting Lynx fans. That stung.

Anyway, you heard from a relative who teaches and coaches in the area that over the years a lot of parents have transferred their kids from North to suburban schools like Centennial and Valley and Dowling Catholic. Then you think how those "Race/Ethnicity" statistics might play with certain kinds of parents looking to "find the right school for their family," exercising their "school choice." You think that maybe for some of those parents "fits right" means "more white."

And then you think, *oooh*, that rhymes.

All of that is interesting, informative, but then you're wondering what that has to do with tonight's game. On a whim, you decide to look up your high school on *GreatSchools.org*. You take note that although AL and North are about the same size, there is a major difference: your school is predominantly white. As in, 82 percent white. Those are almost Centennial numbers. You look at the other ranking categories, however, and see that they are pretty similar to North's, pretty bad. "Very Concerning." You keep searching the data. One of the final categories is percentage of students at AL who come from low-income families and it's around half.

Maybe that's your friends. Maybe that's you.

Either way, it's a lot of poor kids compared to the rest of the state. What about Des Moines North? You go back to the data and see that they have even more students from low-income families: 85 percent. You think of some of the friends you had in elementary school who have since transferred across town to Lewis Central or St. Albert Catholic. And you wonder if for some of those parents "fits right" might also mean "less poor."

That's a discouraging thought. Especially since it doesn't rhyme.

But you're not yet satisfied—you want to push it to the limit, as Coach always tells you to do. You wonder why teams with a lot of poor city kids like North and AL are playing schools with a lot of wealthy suburban kids like Dowling Catholic, Centennial, and Valley. You discover another statistic, that since 2009, in football, Des Moines Public School teams like North are a combined 0–102 against these wealthier suburban schools in the same metro area. The average score of those losses is 50–10.

Your own team, as you well know, has also been fed raw to these suburban Des Moines powerhouses. Over the last three seasons, your

record against them is 0–6, losing by an average score of 58–9. They
rack up a lot of statistics against your team and North's. They get a lot
of athletic scholarship offers on top of all the academic scholarships
(thanks to those high test scores) on top of all the family wealth scholarships (thanks to "school choice").

You, in contrast, rack up a lot of losing. A lot of injuries. Some of
those are more than skin deep.

OK, let's say your composition process kind of stalls out here. You
decide to go back to your original freewrite about Polar Bears to see if
you can jumpstart things, but you're running out of time before the
big game. So you just pick out three maybe-related items among the
scribbles to type into Google—environmental disasters, poverty, vulnerable—and BAM!, a whole lot of new stuff pops up. Too much really,
so you just jot down a few things that you promise to look into later:

Boxing Day tsunami/Indonesian coastal villages. 2004.
Hurricane Katrina/Orleans Parish. 2005.
Drought-induced famine/Sahel Region, Africa. 2010.
Lead-poisoned drinking water/Flint, Michigan. 2014–
Dakota Access Pipeline/Standing Rock Indian Reservation. 2016.
Hurricane Maria/Puerto Rico. 2017.
Arctic warming/Inuit peoples. Ongoing.

This list maybe causes you to think about examples closer to home,
like how the Missouri River seems to flood almost every other year
now, and how the people whose houses are destroyed are mostly in the
poorer areas of your town and other towns, like tiny Pacific Junction,
where the uninsured family of one of your friends lost everything. *Everything.* That doesn't pop up on your keyword internet search, but
you add it to your list anyway.

Wow, you think—that's a lot to fit into a pregame pep talk! You now
have all these strong feelings and opinions and ideas floating around in
your head, and you're not sure where to go with them. It's getting all

mixed up and crazy. You try a couple of lines out, such as "If Environmental Disaster vs. Poor People was a football game, the score would resemble last year's blowout against Des Moines Dowling!" Or "Isn't it ironic that Des Moines North's mascot is a giant white predator?" But they seem a little forced. Now you feel paralyzed. You're beginning to doubt Peter Elbow.

But here's a little secret from the pros: sometimes you spend all this time researching and writing and thinking and feeling and talking and, really, it all comes down to one word. Something that kind of brings it all together. Something to really play for.

So let's do just that. On three ... *for Justice!*

Final Score: Lynx 30 – Polar Bears 16

FINAL GAME: *Council Bluffs Thomas Jefferson High School, October 19, 2018*

First of all, congrats on the big win last week! Yes, go ahead and give yourselves a hand, even though one of your linebackers (who will remain anonymous) informed me that, thanks to my big speech on justice, a number of you are also feeling kind of guilty. That's OK. Guilt can be a powerful motivator for change, especially for privileged, normally oblivious white people from my generation playing the American Game of Life. In their book, a win is a win—why bother with a conscience?

Your generation is going to be different, I totally believe that. Like I believe in this team!

So back to getting rid of that big goose egg on your record. That's a metaphor by the way, not a simile, and I've always wondered about it—I mean, why not an egg laid by a raven or a Komodo dragon or an ant queen? Why privilege the goose? Anyway, the egg is gone—cracked, cooked, and eaten for breakfast in the golden light of a victorious and sort of guilty feeling, yet also newly conscientious, dawn! As

Coach said in the paper, and I quote: "Hopefully winning a football game will start to get the ball bouncing our way a little bit more.... Ideally, we play hard and win this week, and head into the off-season feeling a little better."

I'm not sure what else of substance I can add to those wise and audacious words, but here on the eve of your final game, I'll do my best. As always.

I agree with Coach about heading out of this season feeling a little better about yourselves. For some of you, there will be another shot at a winning season next year. But for the eight seniors, including the Swedish guy, this is it. The final game. For them, the off-season is a little something you may have heard of, called ... *The Rest of Your Life!*

That's bigger than any football game, even if the opponent is the LC Titans, am I right?

And though some of you may be relieved to see this season end, and even more relieved for these pep talks to end—especially Captain Ben—I want to let you know that I'm not leaving you. *Ever.* As anyone will tell you, I'm loyal to a fault. For instance, the starting tight end on my Fantasy Football team, the Prairie Dogs, is Jack Doyle of the Indianapolis Colts. Although he has spent most of the season injured or mired in ineptitude, and has lost my team at least two games, I haven't released him. That loyalty to Jack, that faith, may never lead to a league championship, but I know it has made me a better human being.

But I'm not here to talk about fantasies. As the story of this football team ends, I'm here to invite you to join another team, a real-life team on which I am sometimes the starting quarterback and sometimes the embittered water boy, depending on my mood.

Team Perseverance!

Oh sure, you think, after lecturing us all season about bullies, forced deportations, climate change, species extinction, racism, economic and educational injustice, and chronic traumatic encephalitis, now suddenly you're Mr. Rose-Colored Glasses. *Mr. Hope.* I get it. You're not alone in thinking I can be a little negative at times. Ben's nine-year-old brother says that during the evening news I turn into "The Depress-Ness Monster." That's a reference to the legendary creature in Scotland's Loch Ness, which, by the way, at least one cryptozoologist believes may have died due to the impacts of global warming on the lake's water temperature.

Anyway, Team Perseverance! One of your linebackers (who will remain anonymous) asked me over dinner recently, "Yeah, I understand the world is going to crap, but what can I actually do about it?"

That's a good question. I've asked it myself. And I'd venture to guess so have the guys you are facing on the other side of the ball tonight, from Council Bluffs Thomas Jefferson High School. The Yellow Jackets players, as you're well aware, are from this same community and a public city school very much like your own. *GreatSchools.org* designates them "Very concerning." As it happens, I actually grew up in a similar community and school district, with similar concerns. When I was your age, all I ever wanted to do was leave the "heartland" for some place where I thought my heart would feel more at home—artistically, environmentally, politically. Some place where the ol' Broaster could use his particular skills to help win a game or two for the good guys!

I've since learned that such feelings aren't unusual for young people, or even fifty-year-olds, wherever they live. But if the Depress-Ness Monster teaches us anything, it's that there is no escaping the problems of the world—or the guilt that comes with knowing you have perpetuated more than a few of them. So you might as well start trying to be helpful in the place where you are standing. No matter what anyone tells you, your home is worthy of the best you have to offer.

And keeping it real: home should show some gratitude in return!

I do not say this to encourage arrogance, but because I believe no community should take for granted the passion and talents of its people, young or old. That might begin with giving everyone gift packs like the kind football players receive when they go to bowl games. Something with local flavor, such as a free pass to a casino buffet or a packet of milkweed seeds or, I don't know, affordable health care and a living wage. And a flex helmet.

But even if such gift packs existed, I guarantee you would still experience stretches of crushing doubt. Moments when you don't think you and your particular talents are up to the task ahead—especially if that task is a more just and healthier world. That's when it will be most tempting to hang up the cleats and buy a big box of Orville Redenbacher's "Ultimate Butter" microwave popcorn and binge watch all six seasons of *House of Cards*. Three times.

During those very low points, how do we keep going with the helpfulness? How do we *persevere*?

One winning play you might borrow from us literary pros is to imagine yourself into someone completely different. Maybe someone on a legendary adventure—isn't that pretty much the definition of life? Maybe insert yourself into a favorite book or movie or myth. Or maybe write imaginary letters in which you say all the things you've ever wanted to say on a subject, sounding (as people may have told you) more articulate than you actually are in person.

You can also draw inspiration from heroes. I have a lawyer friend, for instance, who during a bad bout with clinical depression, sometimes imagined himself into Clarence Darrow in order to get out of bed in the morning. No matter if it was a routine estate case or a criminal trial, in his mind he had a court date to defend evolution itself—his own and humanity's.

Or the hero could be nonhuman. Lichen, for instance. Did you know that lichen isn't one creature, but a bizarre fusion of fungus and algae and maybe a few other creatures? Each still has a vital role to play, but because they mutated and joined forces, they are able to live almost anywhere, endure almost anything. It kind of amazes me there aren't more football teams named after them.

Or maybe you can just be yourselves, a bunch of boys on a losing football team from a disadvantaged school district.

That sounds bad, but hang with me a second. Let's start with the boy stuff. You'll hear people say that being a boy is a privileged and powerful thing—and it certainly can be. But somehow, for very real reasons, some of which I may have mentioned in past pep talks, it doesn't feel that way to a lot of you. For all your supposed strength, you feel helpless, even hopeless. You don't know where to go with these feelings, because as a boy you aren't supposed to have feelings.

Maybe you follow my tip and do a little freewriting and research on the subject and discover that, worldwide, the majority of those under-performing in school are boys. You may also discover that between the ages of fifteen and nineteen, boys are three times more likely to kill themselves than girls—four and a half times more likely between the ages of twenty and twenty-four. You discover, or maybe already know, that the vast majority of mass shooters and terrorists and prisoners are boys or former boys.

In explaining these tragic realities, some people will, with good reason, point to culturally reinforced, toxic ideologies about masculinity or domestic violence or dead-beat dads or racism or the mostly male cult of American gun worship. Some might even point to football.

And maybe they're right. Maybe football is a symptom of this larger violence problem for boys. Maybe boys, and the population at large, will be in a better place without it. But here's what I've concluded from watching you guys every week (except for the game at Urbandale, which I've already apologized for missing).

You are *my* heroes!

Yes, I see Blutowski over there sticking his finger down his throat, but just hear me out. All season, I've read or watched stories about victorious high school teams in our area, complete with player highlights and interviews, as if winning is the most difficult and praiseworthy thing a person can do. What you've proven all season is that, even without the winning, you are willing to show up and work when others have surrendered and fled.

That is the definition of perseverance, boys, and it is a big part of the legacy of the 2018 Abraham Lincoln football team, even if no one out there cares to acknowledge it.

Too often, we lend our talents and vision to those who do not need or value them or offer us any gift packs in return. Sometimes those people live elsewhere; sometimes they are our neighbors and family members and so-called friends. Our nation, even. That's how it will always be. But whether you know it or not, this season has taught you to flourish, together, inside what the literary pros call "paradox": courage and despair, strength and vulnerability, faith and doubt, promise and peril.

In a way, paradox defines what it means to be a midwesterner, a bioregion where extremes, even without the climate change, have always come together—in the sky, on the earth. Think tornadoes or lime Jell-O with green olives. It is up to each of us to determine whether that coming together will ultimately be destructive or redemptive.

A victory or a loss, in the truest sense of the word.

So, yes, you are my heroes. And though I can't promise you much, I can promise you this: you will never be alone. No matter the impossible task or dream or quest, inside or outside your head, you will always be among teammates.

This is a truth, unfortunately, that you will forget and have to relearn many times over. These teammates will sometimes be (like me) unexpected, even unwanted. Some will look like you, some won't. They will be both near and far, known and unknown—alive in the past, present, and future. Alive in this locker room, right now, and soon enough, in memory. Imperfect but good people who are bound to you by the fragile selves and communities and planet we share. Bound, as well, by the vow of all committed love: To be there. To try.

Where's the heart in the heartland, you ask? *Beating inside your chest!*

So let's bring it in one last time, boys, for all time. On three ...

For Faith and Love and Justice!

For Hard Work and Helpfulness and Perseverance!

For Home and Heroes!

For Jack Doyle!

For Us!

MY WORKOUT TESTIMONIAL IN THE TIME OF COVID (AND CONCLUSION)

Pizza Night on Planet Fitness

Chris Rondeau, CEO
Planet Fitness Headquarters
4 Liberty Lane West
Hampton, NH 03842

March 2, 2020

Dear Mr. Rondeau,

It is the first Monday of the month and I am once again attending free pizza night here at the local Planet Fitness (aka "No Judgment Zone"), where I have been a member for six years.

I was particularly intent on attending tonight because I do not know how long it will be before I return. Although there are currently no confirmed cases of COVID-19 in Nebraska or Iowa, rumors are that it may soon lead to mass hospitalizations and business closings and major alterations in our lifestyles, including limiting contact with places (like this) where human beings freely touch the same surfaces, exchanging sweat, spittle, high-fives, and more than a few tears. And pizza.

I am not writing to debate closing your doors—I know the decision will be a hard one, or, if the threat continues to rise, no decision at all.

I'm writing only to explain what this night, this place, has meant to me and perhaps a few others it has served.

But first let me say something about this pizza, which is smelling really good right now. It looks like the teenaged attendant ordered a nice variety tonight—pepperoni, sausage, veggie, even a gluten-free option. My favorite is the supreme, and it's seriously calling to me. No Hawaiian, as usual, which has always disappointed my wife when she's attended First Mondays, but you can be forgiven for that. The concept of pineapple as a topping has always been a little controversial.

Sort of like serving pizza in a health club.

I confess I had mixed feelings when Planet Fitness first came to town. You replaced the Barnes & Noble, which had occupied this space for about a decade. When my books came out, I gave readings here to local people, mostly those who knew me personally, mostly elderly, some of whom have since passed away. I miss them. They were from a generation that valued books enough to purchase them. They didn't shop online, but at stores like this Barnes & Noble, which was the only store in our town to stock my books, because it was the only bookstore.

Funny, I used to think of the mega-bookstores as the villains, push-ing out the smaller independent sellers that I still love, but then they were pushed out of business by Amazon. I miss all the physical books that use to inhabit this place and the massive magazine stand and, in the café, the scent of espresso and the panorama of famous authors that made you think you were invited to sit among them. I'd give any-thing right now to join the table with Nabokov and Orwell.

But it's more than that.

When this space was a bookstore, my young sons played at the table with the Thomas the Tank Engine track (talk about germs!) be-neath the Winnie-the-Pooh Hundred Acre Woods panorama, which was where the leg press machines are currently located. Later the boys dressed up as Harry Potter and Ron Weasley for the grand re-lease party of the final Harry Potter book. In the general vicinity of the ab-crunchers, they sat and drank butterbeer, flicking their wet straws at one another and laughing at the big bearded man dressed as Hagrid, but not because he was overweight—already this was a No Judgment Zone. The place was crowded and overheated, and people were breathing all over one another, but even then I thought: *When will we ever see such a spirited, sticky gathering of generations to celebrate the release of a physical book?*

Now this entire section of the mall is set to be demolished and replaced with a Menards.

Even though you've committed to moving only a short distance away, I'm still grieving the loss of the mall. In its prime, it contained not just the bookstore, but other places that meant something to us: the movie theatre and the KB Toys and the holiday Santa display and the video arcade and the glow-in-the dark mini-golf course and the ice cream store and the lily pond–themed play area, where the kids climbed barefoot on the backs of frogs and drooled on giant dragonfly wings, while we sat and took pictures.

We were totally in love with those children. All of them.

The frogs are gone now, but the spongy carpeted area is still there, along with the unimpressive gray tiles. On these same tiles, unchanged during our years here, our boys toddled at first, holding our hands, then ran to and from our arms. Countless reps.

To watch a child grow up has its joys, but it can also feel like a kind of death. A double death when the physical places those children used to inhabit also disappear. Sometimes, when I am doing another set on the leg press, I think I hear a train whistle and the voices of those little boys. Sometimes I think I see them running at me, and the weight I'm lifting with my legs is their bodies and I'm carrying them. Then I snap out of it, due to knee pain, and find myself once again alone with my body.

So change can be hard.

On the other hand, despite chasing and lifting kids, I was pretty unhealthy during most of those early years as a parent, neglecting regular exercise and good eating. I consumed a lot of pizza. I was also in the early stages of trying to support a growing family, and failing at it. I was full of self-judgment. Then, at age thirty-nine, I suffered what my doctor called a stress-induced "cardiac event." I decided I needed something more than my ancient dumbbell set and searched for a health facility I could afford.

For a while, I worked out with my students at our old campus recreation center, alternating sets with them at the bench press. They were very kind, never snickering as they removed most of the weights when it was my turn or when I farted while straining to complete that final rep. When our university decided to build a state-of-the-art recreation center, I got my hopes up. But then it was announced that faculty were required to pay way more than the old fee, which meant it became inhabited mostly by university administrators and professors in colleges like Business, Engineering, and Information Science & Technology. They are, as a result, a remarkably fit looking group. Those of us in the Liberal Arts were left to dig out our nappy sweatsuits from grad school and hit the nearby Elmwood Park playset, waiting in line for three-year-olds to finish their reps on the monkey bars.

I was discouraged.

Then Planet Fitness arrived. Frankly, I hated the purple and gold colors, which resembled the bruises my ego would no doubt develop in such a place. Yes, I heard it was affordable, which is important in our town—due to high poverty levels, all school kids get free lunch here, which often includes pizza—but I still resisted because of the whole workout club culture thing. An allergy that started with Richard Simmons and Olivia Newton-John in the 1980s.

But then, while I was eating a sauce-dripping gyro in what was left of the mall food court (now entirely empty), I peered through the glass wall at everyone exercising. I saw quite a few bodies my own age and disposition. Some of them had this kind of deer-in-the-headlight look, mouths slack, not at all fit looking or in command of their bodily functions. I could relate.

Most persuasive, however, was the familiar woman I spotted on the stepping machine, which as you know is super tall and works kind of like a self-propelled escalator that doesn't take you anywhere. I knew her from the public library, where she often brought her five young kids, unleashing them on the shelves of children's DVDs, which they nearly stripped bare. One of them literally grabbed a Thomas the Tank Engine disc out of my hand. This mom did her best to keep them under control, scolding them occasionally, red-faced, avoiding eye contact with other patrons, but inevitably she would retreat to some other, quieter section of the library and let the kids run amok.

I was kind of judgmental of her, I admit. But seeing her elevated above the fray, queen-like, on the stepping machine, in her royal blue sweatpants and mismatched camo t-shirt, gasping for life while I ate a giant dripping gyro, I was filled with something that might be called admiration.

I took advantage of the "New Year's Resolution Special" ($1 down!) and joined. My first night on the treadmill, I dialed up the soundtrack for *Saturday Night Fever*, and started right in on a heavy sprint, skipping the warm-up because I thought I had to make up for lost time. Half-way through "You Should Be Dancin' (Yeah!)," I sprinted for the toilets. Part of it was that I was out of shape, but it was also because I'd read some internet story about chocolate milk being a great pre-workout protein drink and had guzzled a beer mug full of it just before arriving.

So, although I did indeed yack during my first night at Planet Fitness, I did not do so entirely because my muscles had atrophied, which gave me hope. Hope is good.

As a new member, I mocked First Monday Pizza Night, along with Second Tuesday Bagel Morning, when I first heard about them. Others did, too, as you know. There was a lot of criticism online, some of it fairly justified—I mean, eating pizza seems to defeat the whole purpose, right? So I actually did a little research and discovered that this whole free food thing started in 1998, at your fourth club location in Concord, New Hampshire. The hot water tank had broken down and as a way to thank customers for staying loyal, you offered them free pizza. It soon became a thing, expanding nationwide, along with the chain.

Pizza as gratitude. I liked that.

My research has since uncovered at least one health professional who trumpets the benefits of pizza night. In an interview for *Shape. com*, Sarah Mattison Berndt, MS, RD, stated: "When you train hard, it's only natural to reward yourself from time to time, even if that means post-workout pizza. Although a savory slice provides extra calories and isn't the cleanest recovery fuel, noshing on pizza isn't going to nullify all of your hard work if you aren't doing it all the time. In fact, it may help you to feel more satisfied and ditch feelings of deprivation that could otherwise build up to a blow-out."

"Feelings of deprivation" is a phrase we might be using a lot more in the years ahead.

As for our particular Planet Fitness, it has never run out of hot water that I know of, but it does frequently run out of hand sanitizer. Given the recent national shortages, I don't see that coming back soon, like a lot of things that were meant to protect us. I've gotten in the habit now of using the sink in the men's room to wash my hands between "resistance training" and "aerobic training." It seems like the right timing, since my hands have just been all over the bars and pulleys that so many other hands have been all over.

But can the touching, directly or indirectly, ever really be prevented?

For instance, there are no paper towels in the men's bathroom, so we all use the hand blower. On the surface, that seems the environmentally friendly and sanitary thing to do. Recently, though, I read an article about how these blow dryers are so powerful, they suck all the pieces of the human body floating unseen in the air—skin flakes, hair, microscopic particles of urine and feces—and blow it all back onto your hands.

This offers further proof that bathroom stalls and similarly well-meaning contraptions, such as clothing, may afford us some personal privacy, but do not ultimately protect us from intimacy. That might be something else we become nostalgic for in the coming months. Who knows?

This may sound weird, but one of the other indulgences I really cherish about this place, besides the pizza, are the TV sets all lined up like hunting trophies at the top of the north wall. I know that almost every health club has them, but at home I get only digital reception, so coming here feels a little like when I go to academic conferences and watch cable TV all night instead of proofreading my presentation. Sports especially help me ignore the physical pain, unless its golf. I've watched teams win unremarkable games, now forgotten, and world championships. Tennis, basketball, football, bowling, cage fighting, and a gazillion other sports. I've vicariously triumphed in them all. Such imaginary victories may become all too common as the actual competitions are canceled.

On a related note, I like to switch back and forth between FOX News and CNN, which feels like mental wind sprints and not always inspiring. Even so, through that double prism I've observed two presidential election cycles and most major world events of the last six years, including at least three major epidemics. Through my increasingly sore, exhausted musculature, my breathlessness, the suffering of the world became something more than emotional. Not to mention the vicissitudes of the human condition as conveyed in all those game shows and reality shows and cop/doctor/bachelorette shows. And in the fragments of countless movies from every decade of my life.

I'm not alone in wanting to watch—the machines closest to the televisions are always the most popular with my age group. We've breathed it all in together.

But back to this pizza. It's Domino's, as usual, which always makes me happy right off the bat on First Mondays. There's some history to share about this. In college, I basically survived on lukewarm slices purchased at the corner Domino's near my boarding house. In the evening, I would walk home from the library or from a pick-up bas-ketball game with my buddies, or just an aimless walk, body aching pleasantly, and grab a slice of supreme and a liter of Pepsi. The food was cheap, which was good because I was student-poor.

I owned virtually nothing back then—no car, no house, no club membership; just my physical self that was compensation for all that I didn't own and others did, because they didn't have what I had: a youthful body that could run and dance and love and stay up all night and bask in the sun for as long as it wanted and eat and drink what it wanted. Like the first dusting of snow in November or the first combustion engines cruising dirt roads, nothing in this body had yet accumulated to spoil the landscape and cause regret.

So I ate a lot at that Domino's, alone and with friends—so many friends back then—at an inside table under the fluorescent lights after midnight or outside on the curb to watch the setting sun paint the sky. So much pizza. So much youth. Cheap and warm and filling.

Ah, Domino's. It pretty much smells the same, which is wonderful. As I inhale, I can feel that earlier, younger body stir within me, calling, *I am still here. You can find me. If you feed me.* A siren's song, I know, but still it beckons.

I watch as someone finally succumbs. It is the older gentleman with the ponytail and grey Santa Claus beard. He regularly wears jeans for his workouts, held up with a broad leather belt. I first met him last year at the chest machine, of which there is unfortunately only one—many of us time our workouts so we are ready to hit that thing as soon as it opens up. Sometimes we don't even wait for the previous user to wipe it down, but those days may be numbered.

Anyway, I was sitting there trying to select some music on my ear-phones, when he leaned down and asked how many sets I had left. That's midwestern for, "Will you please get the hell off your phone and finish working out your moobs so I can start on my own?"

"Sorry," I said. "I'm just trying to find the right ELO song. I'll be done soon."

He paused.

"I love ELO."

Instant bond. We've given affectionate yet still manly chin jerks at each other ever since. He gives me one now as he gets ready to shove a slice of supreme into his sweat-dripping face. I give him the thumbs-up, which is midwestern for "Godspeed, my friend."

When I look around, I see several other familiar strangers who have been with me from the start. They are my involuntary support posse. I don't know what I would do if I didn't see at least one of them every time I come in here, which is sometimes every other day and sometimes not at all for weeks. They don't judge me for that. However long it has been, we always acknowledge each other in some way, a wave or chin jerk or just a prolonged staring that in any other context would be sort of creepy. We know each other not by our names, but by our faces, our bodies—some of which have transformed dramatically since we first became aware of one another.

I feel a deep affection for them, these bodies. My teenage son, who used to play with toy trains here, once made a snide remark about a "boomer body" in yoga pants taking her sweet time on the chest machine he was waiting to use. I think he was surprised by my harsh reply, for which I later apologized. He's a good kid, but I needed him to know how much I care for these people, my companions. They haven't come here to get toned for spring break or the downtown bar scene, even if both get canceled this month. No, they have come here to save their lives. I will not tolerate any mockery of them.

There is, for instance, the woman with the military tattoos on her arms and the massive scar on her upper left shoulder. She's in her late thirties or so and sings (badly) at the top of her lungs while on the treadmill, punching the air and cheering for herself. She's cheering for all of us and our private victories, on battlefields real or imagined—at least that's how it feels when I'm on a treadmill anywhere near her. It gets me going.

There's another woman about the same age, a former high school athlete whose husband cheated on her with her best friend. Now she comes here with her older brother. The siblings laugh and talk loudly (which is how I know about the husband) and high-five, in between beating the shit out of the twenty-minute workout machines, all of which are colored coward-yellow, like her ex.

There is the fiftyish, interracial gay couple whom everyone seems to know and love. The Black man is tall and lithe and prefers the rowing machines and ellipticals. The white man has a very muscular upper body but thin legs, which is not uncommon for us middle-aged guys whose knees are shot but whose arms are still working, for now. For us, working out the biceps, unlike the quads or the abs, is like eating pizza—a more immediate gratification. The idea that it might still be possible for me to have biceps like him is truly inspiring. One time, near the pull-up machine, this same guy walked over to someone he knew and asked if he could listen to whatever music she was enjoying. She pulled out one of her wireless earphones, which was undoubtedly covered in sweat, and just gave it to him. He put it in his ear and laughed. Then they did a little dance together.

There is another middle-aged couple who doesn't seem to have a lot of money—you can kind of tell these things by the range and brand of workout clothes people wear. I'm sorry to say such comparisons do take place, even in the No Judgment Zone. This couple wears the same loose gray sweatpants and long-sleeved Ocean Pacific t-shirts from the 80s—his is white with pink lettering; hers is pink with white lettering. Both have images of palm trees on the back. They always show up together and will use only the same kind of machines and only if they are side by side (so no chest workout). And they always exercise in sync, same pace and same number of reps and sets. It never changes. Over the last few years, the length and pacing of their exercising has increased—those once tight palm tree t-shirts becoming, on the treadmills, like triumphant flags flapping loosely in the wind—but their ritual has never wavered. Always together, always to the same invisible beat that has bound them from the beginning.

There is a group of young Latino guys who speak rapid Spanish and move together from one machine to the next, taking turns and helping each other with the weight adjustments. If I get behind them, they can slow down my own workout significantly, but I really like hearing the music of their language, the good humor and comradery in their tones, chock-full of the future.

There's a pimply boy, maybe fifteen, who follows around a super buff guy who I infer is the personal trainer his parents have hired for him. The boy is overweight (No Judgment!), and I've heard him mention something about diabetes. Sometimes he looks a little embarrassed, sometimes scared, but whenever he lays back to do the bench press, his trainer kind of whispers to him. *OK, buddy, just one more set, you can do it.* Maybe he whispers because he's just a soft-spoken guy, or maybe because the kid he's trying to help gets yelled at enough in his life. Or maybe because he doesn't want to set off the Lunk Alarm.

The Lunk Alarm!

It's one of my favorite features here, besides First Monday Pizza Night. As you know, it is literally a siren that goes off whenever a "lunk"—usually a muscle-bound white male—bogarts the free weights and/or squat machines and/or grunts loudly while straining and/or clangs massive amounts of weights up and down. This is one of the reasons I have avoided other gyms. They can make us all feel inadequate, these bodies that ripple like sonic waves, veins snaking all over their taut muscles like a map of the Ozarks.

That said, there are times when I've felt the Lunk Alarm was set off prematurely, without a full appreciation of the personal context of the body in violation. For instance, Myron, who is a friend of the family. He's maybe forty and is a long-time weightlifter, ripped from top to bottom. Every now and then, he clanks a few discs and sets off the siren. But did you know that he only has one eye and that his mom died recently from lung cancer? Plus, he's a really nice guy. Just last week Myron brought his aunt along for the first time, who is around seventy and a former smoker like his late mother, her sister. He was very patient and encouraging while coaching his aunt on the machines, even though she sometimes couldn't complete one rep. I overheard her engaging in a lot of self-judgment. She actually started talking to me about it, how her body used to look, what it was once capable of doing, as she and Myron waited for me to finish on the chest machine. She started crying. So I stopped and gave her a hug, even though we were both pretty sweaty, and she hugged me back and asked God to bless me.

Maybe I'll be telling my grandchildren *this is what it was like in before-COVID times.*

Speaking of someone who might need a hug, there is an octogenarian woman who is bent nearly in half from, I assume, osteoporosis or rheumatoid arthritis. She comes here alone and slowly makes the rounds on almost all the weight machines, in addition to the treadmill—an act of incredible endurance. An example to all. And yet, on the way out, I often hear her ask the young attendant, whoever it is, if she might "please" have one of the grape chew candies in the bucket up front, even though there are plenty and they are free. She knows this and yet she makes a point of asking permission of this young person, who can't possibly know what she's been through the previous hour or near-century. Nevertheless, they always talk for a few minutes before she goes on her way.

I don't want to get anyone in trouble, but there's a teenager here tonight who is on his third slice. Some of my fellow Boomer Bodies are giving him judgmental looks. Personally, I think he and the other teenagers should be allowed to eat as much pizza as they want. In fact, you should encourage them to do so, if you don't already. Our job at this age is to feed them, because that's always been the job of people our age, or should be.

So I want to correct a false impression I might have left earlier, when I called out my son for his momentary frustration with someone from my generation. As COVID-19 has spread, I've heard a lot of critical terms thrown around about his generation—reckless, indifferent, narcissistic. "Health privileged" is a new favorite. *Privileged* is not a term I associate with most of them. For a variety of reasons we can lay right at the feet of people our age, they're mostly poor, or will mostly be poor. I'm not just talking about money. We've left them vulnerable to the future in ways we can hardly understand, since we won't live to see it.

And yet, despite all the ways we've let them down, when the occasional homeless person from my generation comes here on First Mondays to eat some pizza and use the shower, without officially checking in, these same young people invariably turn a blind eye. They pick up their wet towels. They feed them. This makes me love their generation even more than I already do. I'm afraid that in future centuries, when the hot water and a lot of other things run out, we won't be able to send them a pizza of gratitude. So let them have as much as they want right now, OK?

But what is the pizza exactly? What does it *mean*?

Surely, it is more than its individual toppings or crust style. Is it about self-reward? Self-denial? Whatever it means, it cannot be escaped. Not on First Monday Pizza Night. Wherever you go in the club, you will smell it, even if you don't eat it. Even if they provide, as they do, veggie and gluten-free options. It smells the same, like whatever it is you think you need—youth, courage, health, compassion. Food. The pizza will not be ignored or forgotten. It sings. If consumed, it will do inside whatever work it was meant to do, according to the age and composure of the body that consumes it. According to what that body has accomplished (or not) over the last hour or decades—whether completing an additional set of fifteen reps on the arm curl or passing a kidney stone or a baby.

Each slice of pizza, no matter what, will transmogrify into something entirely different inside each of us. A tightening bicep or a loosening layer of belly fat, a self-gratification or self-flagellation. Hate or love, or the memory of love. How many lifelong relationships—friendships, marriages—as well as impulsive carnal mistakes were facilitated by pizza?

Pizza, for some of us, has revealed new worlds. In college I once consumed a slice with sausage and magic mushrooms, and it changed my perception of the color green forever. It changed, as well, the possibilities of what I thought a face might become to another face, in perpetual metamorphosis, in waking dream. As beautifully warped and fleeting as a spring rain on a candlelit window.

That is the human face, compared to what resides, eternal, behind it. That is pizza.

Still, it is becoming clear that COVID-19 will change our lives forever. I worry about my friends here, and their loved ones—as well as my own. When will we see each other again, if ever?

I do not know, but it seems likely that, at the very least, this pandemic could lead to the permanent termination of First Monday Pizza Night. If so, and if we return, I would humbly suggest ordering the pizza anyway and keeping it behind the counter. The smell alone might temporarily overcome the stench of hand sanitizer and fear, becoming a reminder of what we used to mean to one another, freely exchanging the sweat of our struggles, wordlessly confessing the otherwise secret longings and courage of our souls. Demonstrating, for all to see, the possibility of individual and collective morphogenesis, like leaves, because all is leaf—our bodies becoming the place where new growth sprouts from the point of separation from earlier selves, once thought inseparable.

So, yes, the pizza tonight smells good and is loaded with essential meaning, but I have decided to deny myself—a small sacrifice ahead of larger ones to come. Maybe it will leave more for the teenagers.

I will instead dial up Led Zeppelin on the earphones and then, perhaps for the last time in a while, join my fellow human beings, my loves, on the stepping machines. Perhaps for the last time in a while, we shall savor breathing in close proximity the scent that calls to our common hunger. Our bodies going through the motions of what we should know as an absolute truth, whether we recognize it or not, that we are like that married couple, always in perfect sync with one another. Always climbing, together, the stairway that never quite leads to heaven.

Trying to save ourselves with each breathless step.

Affectionately yours,

John Price

ACKNOWLEDGMENTS

So much gratitude to express. Beginning, as always, with my family. They have not only offered me their love and encouragement, but, in some cases, allowed me to write about their lives. I have done my best, however imperfectly, to honor that gift. This includes my parents, Tom and Sondra Price, and my sisters—Carrie Anne, Susan, and Allyson— and their families. Also, my Strine family, especially Gary and Hona. Most of all, Stephanie and our sons, Benjamin, Spencer, and Alden. The love I feel for you all is beyond the measure of words.

At the remarkable University of Iowa Press, I wish to thank my visionary editor and friend, Holly Carver, as well as James McCoy, Meredith Stabel, Susan Hill Newton, Karen Copp, Tegan Daly, and Ann DeVita. Thanks, as well, to my agent, Joanne Wyckoff, for her crucial help and insights.

I was fortunate to work with great editors on earlier, published versions of some of these essays, including Dinty Moore at *Brevity*; Ander Monson at *Essay Daily*; Laura Julier at *Fourth Genre*; Chip Blake, Sumanth Prabhaker, and Jennifer Sahn at *Orion*; and Simmons Buntin and Elizabeth Dodd at *Terrain.org*. An earlier version of "Concerning This Exceptional Research Project" was published in the spring 2019 issue of *Orion Magazine*. "The Burnt Plane" appeared in the fall

2015 issue of *Brevity*. "Confessions of a Prairie Lounge Singer" was published on *Terrain.org* on January 4, 2014. "Peacock Beware!" was published on *Terrain.org* on September 2, 2015. "Holidays on Green" appeared as "Sacred & Mundane" in the January/February 2004 issue of *Orion Magazine*. "Appendicized" originally appeared in *Fourth Genre* vol. 20, no. 2 (2018): 129–52, published by Michigan State University Press. "Dear America" was published on *Terrain.org* on May 18, 2017. "Pizza Night on Planet Fitness" was published on *Terrain.org* as "Pizza Night on Planet Fitness: On Love, Sweat and Community in the Time of Coronavirus" on March 23, 2020. "On Hoagland, Turtles, and the Courage of Simile" was published on *Essay Daily* on December 23, 2013.

Perhaps more than any other book I've written, I relied on the advice, help, and good will of friends. These include Karla Armbruster, Karen Bergquist Lueth, Lance Brisbois, Taylor Brorby, Simmons Buntin, Chris Cokinos, Clinton Crocket Peters, Cindy Crosby, Christina Dando, Janine DeBaise, Elizabeth Dodd, Hope Edelman, Cristina Eisenberg, Kristin Girten, Angela Glover, Chad Graeve, David Hamilton, Will Jennings, Al Kammerer, Tina Kneisel Bakehouse, Jeff Koterba, Merloyd Lawrence, Tom Lynch, Matt Mason, Michael McDermott, Corey McIntosh, Sarah McKinstry-Brown, Kathryn Miles, Nick Monk, Susan Naramore Maher, Andy Nesler, Doug and Julie O'Riley, Lanette Plambeck, Glenn Pollack, Tina Popson, Joseph Price, Dave Rintoul, Suzanne Roberts, Barbara Robins, Todd Robinson, Michael Skau, Chris St. Clair, Aubrey Streit Krug, Ned and Elizabeth Stuckey-French, George and Sheila Sturm, Mary Swander, Alan Weltzien, and Scott Working.

For their extra-generosity in offering essential information, research and other critical support, I'd like to doubly thank these friends: Isabel Barros, Katie Bishop, Tom Bragg, Eryn Branch, Sara Dohrmann, Barbi Hayes, Brian Hazlett and Ryan Allen (at Briar Cliff University's Center for Prairie Studies), Chuck Johanningsmeier, Lydia Kang, Carl Klaus,

Eric Konigsberg, John and Barb McKenna, Michele Morano, Connie Mutel, Dave Pantos, Jack Phillips, Daryl Smith, Kathleen Thompson, Mike Whye, Sue William Silverman, and everyone at the Black Earth Institute.

I owe a special debt to Michael Branch, Tom Montgomery Fate, and Elmar Lueth for their unwavering acts of kindness and good humor. So, too, my dear friends in the Moll Frith Society—Dan Boster, Jeff Garst, Jeff Lacey, Matthew Marx, David Peterson, and Kyle Simonsen—who provided companionship, laughter, and good pipe tobacco during challenging times.

Many thanks to my friends and colleagues at the University of Nebraska at Omaha for their ongoing support. These include English Department Chair Tracy Bridgeford and Dean of the College of Arts and Sciences Dave Boocker. Also, my creative nonfiction compadres, Jody Keisner, Tammie Kennedy, Lisa Knopp, Aero Rogers, and Kyle Simonsen. Thank you to Yvette and Doug Kinney for their generous support of our creative nonfiction faculty and students. Thanks, as well, to Kevin Clouther and Richard Duggin of the University of Nebraska Low-Residency MFA, and Steve Langan of the UNO Medical Humanities Program. Dustin Pendley and Jill Sutton, you have helped me too many times to count—the cacti and I are eternally grateful.

Finally, I'd like to dedicate this book to the memory of my dear friend and teacher, Carl Klaus. And to my students, you continue to inspire me to learn, to grow, and to hope. Write on.

SELECTED BUR OAK BOOKS

All Is Leaf
John T. Price

The Biographical Dictionary of Iowa
by David Hudson, Marvin Bergman, and Loren Horton

A Bountiful Harvest
by Leslie A. Loveless

Central Standard
by Patrick Irelan

The Emerald Horizon
by Cornelia F. Mutel

Enchanted by Prairie
photographed by Bill Witt

The Folks
by Ruth Suckow

Fragile Giants
by Cornelia F. Mutel

Green, Fair, and Prosperous
by Charles E. Connerly

Hidden Prairie
by Chris Helzer

An Iowa Album
by Mary Bennett

The Iowa Nature Calendar
by Jean C. Prior and James Sandrock

Landforms of Iowa
by Jean C. Prior

Man Killed by Pheasant and Other Kinships
by John T. Price

Of Men and Marshes
by Paul L. Errington

Of Wilderness and Wolves
by Paul L. Errington and Matthew Wynn Sivils

Out Home
by John Madson and Michael McIntosh

Picturing Utopia
by Abigail Foerstner

A *Place of Sense*
edited by Michael Martone

Prairie City, Iowa
by Douglas Bauer

A *Ruth Suckow Omnibus*
by Ruth Suckow

State Fair
by Phil Stong

Stories from under the Sky
by John Madson

A Sugar Creek Chronicle
by Cornelia F. Mutel

Sunday Afternoon on the Porch
photographed by Everett W. Kuntz
text by Jim Heynen

The Tallgrass Prairie Reader
edited by John T. Price

To Find a Pasqueflower
by Greg Hoch

Townships
edited by Michael Martone

Up on the River
by John Madson

Where the Sky Began
by John Madson

Wildland Sentinel
by Erika Billerbeck